Chetham's

OLD AND NEW IN HARMONY

The choir and orchestra (soloist Michael Rippon) conducted by
Michael Brewer in *Belshazzar's Feast*, Free Trade Hall, 5 July 1986

PENRY WILLIAMS

Chetham's

OLD AND NEW IN HARMONY

Manchester University Press · Chetham's

Published for Chetham's School of Music
by Manchester University Press,
Oxford Road, Manchester, M13 9PL, UK
27 South Main Street, Wolfeboro, NH 03894-2069, USA

British Library cataloguing in publication data
Williams, Penry
   Chetham's : old and new in harmony.
   1. Chetham's School of Music — History
   I. Title
   780'.7'2942733   MT5.M272C44

Library of Congress cataloguing in publication data
Williams, Penry
   Chetham's : old and new in harmony.
   1. Chetham's School of Music 2. Music—Instruction
   and study—Great Britain. I. Title.
   MT3.G7W47   1986   780'.7'294273   86-18259

ISBN 0-7190-1973-7 *paperback*
ISBN 0-7190-2380-7 *hardback*

Printed in Great Britain
by Bell and Bain, Glasgow

02203998 PΦ

Contents

List of illustrations   vi
Foreword by *Yehudi Menuhin, KBE*   vii
Beginnings   1

1   *Blue Coat boy*   3

2   *Education at the Hospital School*   29

3   *The war years*   45

4   *Grammar School*   57

5   *Music before 1969*   72

6   *Why a music school?*   85

7   *Years of difficulty*   94

8   *Audition and settling-in*   107

9   *Music School*   120

10   *Specialism*   134

Appendices
1   The origin of Mr Humphrey Chetham's
    Hospital School and its operation under
    the terms of his 1651 will   141
2   School uniform   156
3   Visitors   157

List of illustrations

A petition, 1857   *page* 4

The Library Reading Room   The 'Baronial Hall'   23

The school buildings   24, 25

Tossing the pancake   In the workshop   26

The morning ablutions   27

Midday meal, 1956   Dormitory   28

'General Routine' at Chetham's Hospital   30

Cricket before 1900   Football in the 1930s   69

The Chetham's brass band   The choir, 1956   70

Humphrey Chetham presiding over the ruins
Founder's Day procession   71

Relaxation   A new bedroom (photo Barry Gardiner)   117

Wind trio with Lady Barbirolli
Brass master-class with Philip Jones   118

The school orchestra, 1970
The Studio (photo Arthur Taylor)   119

Belshazzar's Feast, 1986 (photo Ian Gee)   *frontispiece*

occasional line drawings by Enid Williams

Foreword

I am thrilled to see a fairy tale come true in the transformation of the Ugly Duckling into the Beautiful Swan – in this case, in the transformation of a dilapidated Dickensian building into one of our foremost musical institutions, one of the most exciting and stimulating artistic developments in this country.

The risks at the outset were great, but the rewards have repaid our confidence, and I am proud to have played a small part in the history of Chetham's.

This book reflects the achievements of a dedicated group of people; it is founded on a love of music which I hope will be passed on to its readers, and will continue to sustain those who will work for the future of a great music school.

Yehudi Menuhin

Beginnings

A beginning there was in 1656 when forty poor boys were provided with a home in old college buildings which had recently been re-roofed and made habitable. Details about the origin of Chetham's Hospital School are set out in Appendix 1. The Hospital was a Puritan foundation where, as well as leading to an understanding of the scriptures, education would be a preparation for responsible work and service within the community. The boys were fed, clothed and prepared for apprenticeship. In a way they were privileged because otherwise they would have to be at work to contribute to the family budget. The basis of the school was to remain virtually unchanged for three centuries.

A second beginning came in 1952. The resources of the endowment had proved insufficient to enable the Hospital School to continue, and it was almost closed down in 1945. However, means were found for the school to change into a boys' grammar school with entry by selective examination, and for the education to concentrate on preparation for careers in the professions. It was as if windows in the old college buildings were being opened to welcome the winds of educational change that were affecting all schools in the post World War II world. The college itself seemed to retain an outward calm and continuity, but within the walls were intense activity and rapid change. Previously, the habit had been to regard children as miniature adults conforming to a set pattern, but now the stress was more on individuality and initiative. The pages that follow record the experience of children as these changes took place.

It was music that led to a third beginning in 1969. Children were to be selected because of their exceptional ability in music. In this country, this was a new venture in education and many questions were raised as to the nature of child growth and the development of special abilities. This book offers no answers to such questions but records what has been happening at Chetham's. Another beginning has been made, and it remains to be seen where the new path will lead.

My thanks are due to all who have helped in the preparation of this book, notably the children I have been privileged to teach during the twenty six years I was at the school. Their experience has been the driving-force to make me record the effect of change as it took place. My thanks are also due to the Governors of Chetham's School and Library for offering me every facility to examine all aspects of the school. I might add that the views expressed are entirely my own and that they are in no way to be held responsible for what is, after all, a personal interpretation. There are many who have generously given of their time in talking of their old times at the school, and have allowed me to use extracts from the tape-recordings that have been made. I would also like to record my thanks to Professor E. J. Evans, University of Lancaster, for his valuable help and advice. Finally, I would not have been able to continue with the work without the support and understanding, to say nothing of the patience, of my wife, whose illustrations provide a valuable insight into life at Chetham's.

P. W.

CHAPTER 1

Blue Coat boy

Seeing a school through the eyes of a child may seem childish, even inappropriate, yet to ignore the child would be unreal. Schools exist for children. Looking back on school days can produce misleading impressions because we remember only happy or miserable moments. Also, such recollections could reflect adult hopes and fears rather than what the young child was experiencing. From seven to fourteen in anyone's life is a vital time of growth. The reconstruction that follows is based on the collective reminiscences of a number of former pupils at Chetham's Hospital School between 1900 and 1939 when the school was evacuated. Care has been taken to avoid what was too particular and unusual, and to concentrate on a general pattern. Pattern there certainly was, because little changed inside Chetham's during the first half of the twentieth century.

Boys were elected to the Hospital School and on leaving were provided with an indenture. Election and indenture had relevance in the seventeenth century, and continued into the twentieth century as a means of entry and leaving the school. Elections depended on vacancies and a vacancy would relate to a particular parish. The list of vacancies would be circularised and notices displayed in parish churches. The clergy and churchwardens would interest themselves in deserving cases and applicants would be invited to attend for election, having already been selected by the parish on grounds of family need, respectability and sound health. A petition form would then be presented.

Elections took place at the Hospital at the Easter and Michaelmas meetings of the governors. It was a selective entry of a careful nature. The wordings of the petition specifically excluded bastards, and there were to be dismissals if false entries were discovered. A reading test excluded boys who would be difficult to teach. The test would also support the

To the GOVERNORS of the HOSPITAL and LIBRARY in MANCHESTER, FOUNDED by HUMPHREY CHETHAM, Esquire, and INCORPORATED by KING CHARLES the SECOND.

Name, Residence, and Occupation of the Parent or Friend of the Boy. *Tebutt*

The Petition of *Caroline Crabtree* of No. *27* Street, in the Town or Township of *Manchester*, in the County of Lancaster,

Manchester, Salford, Droylsden, Crumpsall, Boulton-in-the-Mo rs, or Turton, and not elsewhere.

On behalf of *John Crabtree*, a Poor Boy, an Inhabitant of the Town or Township of *Manchester* who was born in *Tebutt St, Manchester* and was Christened in the Parish Church

Above 6 and under 10 years.

of *St Simon & St Jude* and is now of the Age of *Eight* years and *Three seven* months, or thereabouts, and is the Son of *Richard Jackson Crabtree* and *Caroline* his Wife, "honest, industrious, and painful Parents, and not wandering or idle beggars or rogues, and is not a bastard, nor lame, infirm, or diseased."

State the Names and Ages of all the Children, and Earnings of Children and Parents, if any.

Nathan Crabtree 15 yrs of age, earns 6/ per week
Emma Crabtree 14 yrs of age, assists mother at home
Joseph do 11 yr do earns 3/ per week [at present out of]
Richard do 9 yr do goes to school
John do 8 yr do goes to school
Mary Ann do 6 yr do goes to school
Caroline do 5 yr do do nothing
Catherine do 3 yr do "
Ann do 1 yr do "

State the circumstances of the Parents or Guardians, and any further facts in support of the Petition, and if the Candidate has a Brother in this or any similar Institution.

The Father when living sought earnestly to maintain his large family honestly and bring them up in the path of virtue. He [was] a diligent Sunday School teacher to the last. No other child is in a similar institution.

State the religious persuasion of the Parents or Guardians.

Church of England

CAN THE CANDIDATE REPEAT

Write Yes or No opposite each section.

The Lord's Prayer? *Yes*
The Apostles' Creed? *Yes*
The Ten Commandments? *Yes*
Read the New Testament distinctly? *Yes*

Your Petitioner therefore prays that you will Elect the said poor boy into your Hospital, and admit him to partake of the Charity so far as you shall deem him worthy according to the Rules thereof.

Signed, the *fifth* day of *September* 1857

Signature of Petitioner. Insert the designation.

The mark of *Caroline Crabtree*

We, the *Churchwardens and Overseers* of the Poor of the said Township of *Manchester* or the greater number of them, do hereby Certify that *John Crabtree*

Certificate to be signed by the Churchwardens, Guardians, or Overseers of the Poor of the Town or Township of which the boy is an inhabitant.

the poor boy above-named is an Inhabitant of the said Town or Township of *Manchester* and we believe the facts stated in the above Petition are true.

Witness our hands, the *fifth* day of *September* 1857

Herbert Bailey } Churchwarden
Henry M Ormerod }
Robt Royle Overseer *of Manchr*

N.B.—Should it afterwards be discovered that the Governors have been deceived in any of the foregoing particulars, the Boy admitted under such misrepresentation will be IMMEDIATELY returned to his Parents or Friends.

claim of respectability for the family because the candidate would be asked 'to repeat the Lord's Prayer, the Ten Commandments and the Apostles' Creed and read the New Testament distinctly'. The boys were not necessarily orphans but the sons of families who were facing difficulties. The petition would be endorsed 'by a Clergyman, Churchwarden, Guardian or Overseer of the Poor of the Town or Township in which the Candidate resides'.

Here, seen in retrospect, is an election which took place in 1911.

I suppose circumstances such as mine were quite common in those days. My mother was a monthly nurse and I was left alone quite a good deal. I have two sisters, one was at home and the other was married. The one that was at home did all the work and I was left on my own. You know how you get into mischief and I think that I was beginning to be a problem to mother. Off I went for a religious examination and I was quite pleased with my progress. I had to read the Bible, say the Lord's Prayer, answer the Catechism and recite the Apostles' Creed and the Commandments, which I knew quite well. The next stage was that we must go for an interview in the school. Mother had, of course, in the meantime filled in my application form, I had been examined by a local Doctor and she'd got various people to speak for the application. Being a nurse she was able to get influential people to fill in my petition. When I got to the school we saw quite a lot of parents with their boys. There were only a limited number of vacancies. We were all expecting to get a place, but we found that some of them had applied before. I think the Feoffees in those days considered that if you were very young and there were other applicants older, they gave preference to the older boys rather than the younger boys because they were at the disadvantage of not being able to apply again. I was in that position – I was almost ten when the election was held and it was my first and last application, and I was delighted to be accepted.

The selection process must have been a harrowing experience when a decision had to be made as to which home circumstances were worse than others. 'I was four months short of my tenth birthday. My father died in October 1912 leaving mother with five children, and I was the oldest. This left her in desperate straits for in those days there was no social security, so my mother was grateful to have my brother and

I elected to the College.'

The outbreak of war in 1914 produced a different social problem. 'I really have to start with 1914. When my father died I spent the summer of that year in London with an aunt, a sister of my father, who offered to take me and bring me up. I was out one Sunday afternoon and newspaper specials shouted that war was declared. I went in and told my aunt, but she didn't believe me. I was packed off home to Manchester and I was elected in 1915. Three years later I remember meeting the school barber near the Cathedral and he told me to tell the House Governor than an armistice had been agreed. I did so, but I wasn't believed until it was seen in print. I was right on both occasions. I carried the news about war and the armistice in two entirely different places and was not believed – and I was a very truthful little boy.' Another war-time entry: 'I was baptised when I was nine years old in order to gain entry. A large proportion of the boys had lost their fathers in the 1914-18 war. My mother was a war widow left with five boys and a girl all under the age of ten.'

The pattern of English education was changing and part of this change resulted in a certain stigma being attached to a charity school. 'My father died in July 1925 when he was forty and I was nine years old. My brother was born in September. My mother was told she would have a lot on her hands just bringing up the little baby with no money coming in, but she had her pride. She was my mother, she said, and it was her responsibility to bring me up. She had never heard of Chetham's and at first would not listen. We had a very competent parish priest who had spent forty two years in the parish and knew all the families. He pressurised my mother to let me go in for the next election, but she said 'No' and that she could manage. She didn't want me to go, as she called it, into an orphanage. It was tantamount to going into a workhouse.'

Where there was need and where there was a vacancy, Chetham's could help. 'In 1931 both my parents died. I was born an eighth child in 1923 and there were two more children making ten in all. Three died, leaving seven. My oldest sister aged twenty one and six younger children were left without parents. The three eldest girls worked in the mill on short time, because of the slump of 1926. The eldest son was working in a bleachworks. My sister had a word with the Headmaster of the school I attended and consequently an application was made for me to go to Chetham's.'

Special care was taken over the physical condition of the applicant. The doctor, who would be 'the usual Medical Attendant of the Family', had to certify that the boy was 'exempt from Deformity, and all serious defects, both physical and mental. There exists in him, at present, no infectious disease. Fits and Incontinence of Urine are particularised as amongst the serious defects that incapacitate a child from being placed on the list of candidates.'

The check on personal hygiene became regularised with a compulsory bath night each Saturday. A stone bath was sunk into the floor of the washhouse, and about fifteen boys went into the bath at a time under the supervision of prefects. 'The bath was about four feet deep, heated by steam pipes along the end away from the steps. The steam pumping in made a growling sound and young boys were terrified with the older boys saying there was a crocodile at the other end of the bath. Sometimes the water was so hot that boys who had tender skins came out like boiled lobsters. A long coconut matting was laid from the washhouse to near the fire where the Governor, or sometimes Matron, sat. We went along the mat and showed ourselves to the 'Guv.', presenting hands, turning round and bending down to have our backsides looked at.' (1918) The routine was similar in the 1930s: 'All boys bathed in the same water, plus Jeyes Jelly in the hair, sometimes in the eyes. We were kept warm by the dayroom fire, waiting our turn to be inspected by Governor. His speciality was toe and finger-nails, and any blemishes on the body.' (1938)

Parents and guardians were permitted to see their boys on visiting days, which were strictly rationed and supervised, and other regulations were designed to discourage too close a relationship between the Hospital and a home. 'Parents are requested not to ask for the boys to attend Parties, Funerals, etc. or to visit relatives during term time. Boys are not allowed to visit their homes during term time.' On return after a holiday all boys had to be medically examined to prevent any infection being introduced. 'Boys failing to attend the Medical Examination without leave of absence, will not be re-admitted by the House Governor. Negligence or indifference on the part of the Guardian to conform to the rules may lead to the boy being dismissed from the Foundation.' School Camp took place when boys returned after the summer break, but no boy could go to camp unless he had passed the medical fitness test on his first day back. The constant attention which was given to health contributed to the reputation of the school in turning out hardy boys who could face the rigours of adult life.

On entry each boy was given a number according to his height, the tallest being Number One and the smallest having the highest number. The numbers related to wooden bench-lockers which lined the walls of the Day Room where the boys assembled, and in these lockers were the numbered clothing and such personal property as a hairbrush, toothbrush and a tin of Brasso to polish buttons. When seniors left and new-comers came in at six-monthly intervals, a reallocation of numbers would take place. Clothes for a particular number would be issued to the boy of that number so that a change in number, according to a change in height, would provide clothing previously worn by another boy.

On my first day I had to take off my clothes and put on number 59's clothes. To me, wearing someone else's clothes was an anathema. In the first weekly inspection I marched up to the master-in-charge with number 59's coat on. 'You've got stains down the front of your jacket,' I was told. 'It's not my jacket,' I replied, and was immediately struck around the ears and knocked to the ground. I didn't go down because he hit me so hard, it was probably just the shock of it all. I thought: Right! He is not going to make me cry! So I got up. 'What did you mean by that remark?' he asked. 'It isn't my coat, these are not my things, I didn't put the stain on and I am not going to take it off.' He said: 'You will take that stain off,' and went on to explain that clothes were issued free to everybody and that it was the duty of everybody to keep their clothes clean. After the first shock it made sense to me, but no one had ever knocked me to the floor in an ordinary school. (1926)

The numbering of clothes was to provide an unexpected benefit in later years. 'When we were evacuated, landladies liked having Chetham boys because there were no problems about the washing of clothes. We took our washing to the Memorial Hall at Cleveleys and collected our clean clothes out of hampers. Everyone's had a number on, even down to our stockings. Our landladies didn't have the sort of problems which other landladies had with other evacuees.'

A new boy would have a 'Father', a senior pupil usually from the same parish whose duty was to introduce him to the rules, to advise when any problems arose, and, if necessary, prevent him from being bullied. Bullying never seems to have been carried out at Chetham's, and probably the appointment of a 'Father' for the first six months was a contributory factor. Most of the boys were, in fact, without fathers of their own.

Having been numbered and given a 'Father' the ordeal of a break with home had to be faced. 'During my first year I was terribly homesick being away from my mother for the first time in my life. I went to sleep each night with thoughts of home filling my mind. Being troubled with a sore arm I was not able to join in any of the boisterous games and sports. We were not given anything to read at that time. I often felt lonely, very lonely, and sometimes I felt I was an outsider' (1898). A seven-year-old coming from a friendly and large family would find it difficult to adjust: 'I was the second youngest with a brother and three sisters, and I was just seven when I was elected in 1919. There was a lot of crying went on in the dormitory at night. We consoled each other and by the time you were nine you got used to it. It took that long for it to wear off.'

Much would depend on conditions at home. In some cases it was preferable to be at Chetham's. Contact with home was generally discouraged, except by letter, and visiting days were deliberately restricted. 'I only had one visit from my brother, who called to take me to the funeral of another brother. I used to go out of bounds on visiting days. The fox court was a favourite place, and sometimes I would have a weep and ask God why I couldn't have a mother. On occasions the boys would come and fetch me, and their mothers would insist on giving me sweets and cakes which made me all the more miserable' (1905).

The rising bell would be pulled by the Porter at 6.00 a.m.

The boys put on their stockings and slippers, made their beds, and then stood (shivering in winter) in their shirts at the side of the bed. Pyjamas or night-shirts were unknown: they slept in their day-shirts, which were laundered weekly. Beds were inspected, and any not made tidily enough had to be re-made and a punishment handed out. 'We had a chamber pot between three of us and we emptied it in turn. One boy in my section of three never would empty his pot. He used to push it under my bed so that it was my job next day. They couldn't see it when the bed and quilt were over the top. We would empty them in the toilet in one of the three dormitories. We laid all those empty pots outside. I don't know whether they were washed every day, but we had a dormitory maid who used to wash them one or two times a week and put them back under the beds. We had about thirty chamber pots for the boys, and there was quite a procession of us going down to empty the pots!' (1915).

The Porter and Boiler Man was not resident, but he never failed to start the boys' day at 6.00 a.m. He left his house in Eccles about 4.30 and would clear the boiler and get up steam. He was working at Chetham's before World War I, returned after military service, continued during the inter-war years and his son-in-law took his place in the 1950s until he in turn retired in the mid 1970s. Both men were admired and respected, and occasionally feared, by the boys, and a family connection of this nature, and of so long duration, gave an appearance of durability to the establishment.

The bell-rope runs through a hole in one of the dormitories, now the School Library, down to a passage below. On one occasion, instead of the usual short ring, the rope was pulled for minute after minute. The boy next to the rope jumped out of bed and gave the rope a big tug, jerking it out of the hands of the Porter below. 'Who pulled that rope up?' 'I did,' the boy replied, 'and if you ever ring it like that again, I shall do the same thing again.' 'You can't talk to me like that,' came the reply. 'I shall go straight to the House Governor.' 'Well go to the House Governor, because if you do it again, I shall do it again.' To be woken up by a loud bell which went on and on jangling was not pleasant, but to complain was an act of insubordination which everyone thought would meet with severe punishment. The House Governor, W. J. Fielden, was well known for his discipline and was generally feared for the punishments he administered. The boy was summoned to his presence, but to general surprise instead of chastisement the boy was told that the Porter had left home very early and possibly thought that if he himself was up and about, everyone else should be up and about as well. The story is recalled for two reasons; the unusual leniency shown to the boy, and the spirit of the boy in protesting, even to the House Governor. The teller of the story adds this postscript: 'These boys went to that school because they had nothing. Their parents had nothing. Whenever I go back, I always go to the War Memorial where seventy five percent of the names recorded there were at school with me. His name is among them. I see him as he was when he was about fifteen. He had tremendous spirit. You know when they say at Remembrance Day services: 'They shall not grow old as we that are left grow old.' Well, they don't grow old, do they?'

Having woken the boys up and attended to the boiler, the Porter would slice the bread for the boys' breakfast and supervise the boys who were on duty to put margarine on the bread. After a breakfast break for the domestic staff, the boys' breakfast would be served at 7.30 a.m. At 8.00, having made sure that the boys had tidied the buttery and cleared the tables, he would regulate the fires to make sure there was hot water for cooking and laundry. General maintenance work would occupy him for the rest of the day, but he would serve the boys' lunch at 12 noon, and the boys' tea would be prepared under his supervision from 5.00 to 5.40, and then served. There would follow the usual sweeping and banking-up of the boiler, after which he would depart and be back for the boiler and rising-bell at 6.00 a.m. the next morning.

The boys, after bed inspection, would leave the dormitories and troop downstairs to the washhouse and the numbered wooden boxes. It was now the time for trades. A Trade List set out what each boy had to do. New boys would pick up litter but after six months would be transferred to more specific work. The habit of responsibility for general cleanliness, as well as the fulfilment of a duty, was an essential part of the Chetham's training. The trades system also reduced maintenance costs.

There would be sweeping the flagged path and all the passages. The swimming baths, dormitories, dayroom and cloisters would all need cleaning. The boiler would need to be banked with coke, and boys' toilets would need to be washed out. The House Governor's waste bucket would need emptying, and the Masters' shoes would need cleaning. Or you might be a tracer. 'Sand would be thrown over the flagged floor of the Baronial Hall. You would walk round trailing a soft sweeping brush behind you. It left a pattern of the marks made by the hairs of the brush. Of course, if you didn't get the pattern right, you were for it.'

Up at 6.00 a.m., beds inspected, trades done, it was now time for breakfast. 'I was quite happy on my first morning. I remember distinctly smelling the aroma of bacon and eggs floating about the buildings end of the quadrangle, and I thought that was going to be home from home. The kitchen was almost opposite the Baronial Hall where we ate, but the breakfast of bacon and eggs was being prepared for the teaching staff, who had their meal elsewhere. We only had bread and margarine. I would really like to have seen the expression on my face that morning' (1915).

Breakfast consisted of two rounds of bread, porridge and a jug of tea or cocoa brought round by the Carriers, boys on breakfast duty. The porridge was made with syrup and there was never any sugar or salt on the tables. 'Sometimes it was very lumpy. Bowls were piled up for the Carriers to take away, with the top bowl empty and porridge oozing out of bottom bowls. I have seen the Governor come round and say: 'Who's leaving my porridge?' He would then give out all the bowls again and share out the porridge, and stand and make sure the porridge was eaten'. (1932). Back in 1898 'each boy had a rather thick slice of bread from a loaf baked in the College Bakehouse, thinly spread with margarine, and a cup of tea. Nothing else. There was always great competition for the crusts.'

If you were a friend of one of the Carriers you could get

special pieces of bread spread with thick margarine. Your initials were put in the margarine, and the bread put underneath all the other pieces. 'Now I've seen them play tricks with the boys. Sometimes they got a thick slice of bread, carved the middle out of it, filled it with sand and covered it over. Then they told him: 'We've got a special today, and its on your table.' He'd start eating it and his mouth would be full of sand.' The bread slicing machine could not cut right to the end of the loaf, and a 'Nudger' or 'Tram Stopper' was left, a crust about two inches thick. Nudgers were supposed to be taken in turn, but their distribution was fixed by the buttery boys for their friends, or the Prefect.

You had your own place in the Baronial Hall. In complete silence the House Governor would come down from his quarters, stand at the lectern and morning prayers would begin. He would then give out mail. He had already opened all the mail, read it, and sometimes would read out extracts from one or two letters. He would then depart, leaving the Master on duty in charge. Grace was sung before and after every meal. (Before): 'Lord, Lord, we praise Thee for these great Blessings, provided by our Founder with such paternal care. Through Jesus Christ our Lord, Amen.' (After): 'Relieve, O Lord, the wants of others and give us thankful hearts. Through Jesus Christ our Lord, Amen.' If you were outside the hall the sound of the boys' voices had a special appeal. 'Considering we weren't a musical school then (1930), and that we weren't choristers but just ordinary boys who sang together, there was a sort of discipline and a balance between the older boys and the younger ones which harmonised exceptionally well. But we sang together regularly.'

Tea was the last meal of the day and was the same as breakfast, bread and margarine and a drink, 'but on Sundays we had a piece of madeira cake instead of one of the pieces of bread' (1898 and 1913). Another Sunday exception was an egg for breakfast. Boys who had been confirmed attended the 8.00 a.m. communion service in the Cathedral. 'We lost no time in returning for our Sunday treat, one – or two eggs, if you were lucky.' At 9.00 a.m. there would be a Bible reading in the day-room, and a collect would be read. All would attend Matins at 10.30, and Evensong at 3.00, in full procession 'with no talking allowed en route to the Cathedral and back. No one was allowed to leave the school grounds from the beginning of term to the end except the prefects on special errands. We would walk in the school grounds and sit on forms, weather permitting. At certain times of the year you were kept busy killing cockroaches and shaking them off your clothes' (1931).

An earlier reminiscence from 1905 mentions the sermons in the Cathedral. 'I always enjoyed the services, feeling free from restraint while I was there. I cannot recall any particular sermon, but I am quite sure that my life was providentially influenced by them, particularly by those preached by Canon Peter Green who was noted for his determined opposition to all forms of gambling and for his work among boys. Every Sunday evening we assembled in the dayroom and the Governor read a story to us. Occasionally he would allow one of the senior boys to read a story of his own choosing, but it had first to receive the Governor's approval. Some of us often found more entertainment watching a mouse, followed by a large litter, emerge from a hole in the skirting board, scuttle behind the boxes, then back, time and time again.'

The main meal of the day was at midday, and although the diet may have been monotonous, the general standard of health was good. At their homes it would not have been practicable for the boys to be fed on such a regular basis or so steady a diet. In 1911 the then Headmaster, as distinct from the Governor, would supervise the Monday meal. 'We used to have boiled eggs on Monday brought to us in a basket. Many of them were a bit musty and we used to go up to him and say: 'Please sir, this egg is not good.' We all knew he had no sense of smell, so he used to get one of the senior boys to smell the eggs for him. If the boy said it was bad, you'd get another egg.'

There would be the special 'treat' days. Dr Andrew Boutflower, medical attendant to the school, provided a large simnel cake for mid-Lent on what today would be called Mothering Sunday. It would be sliced into one hundred pieces so that each boy could have one. He also provided treacle toffee and parkin for the Fifth of November Gunpowder Plot celebration. These practices began before World War I and were continued by his widow after he died in 1931 until the mid-1940s. From time to time there would be gifts of fruit from other sources. 'In the summers of 1913-1914 we had what was known as Strawberry Day. On this day we enjoyed a large plate of strawberries given by an Old Boy. It was discontinued by the Governor in 1915. He told the assembled school it was our contribution to the war effort.'

Stews and soups presented difficulties because they were prepared in two copper boilers in the brew house which was infested with beetles. The boilers had half-lids which were held open by a chain. 'It was alleged that the lid was left open during the night and that the following morning the kitchen maid in the bad light put the food in the boiler, lit the gas, and so we had beetle soup. Many boys were sick at the dinner tables having eaten much of the soup before discovering the beetles.' This account dates from 1920 and in the 1930s a regular pastime was to have cockroach races, or competitions to find the biggest. One boy, returning later than the usual 7.30 bed time reports that 'if we went to the brew house, the walls were crawling with them. When you got there they would be on the walls. As you walked towards them it was like a black sheet separating. It was fantastic!'

With a 7.30 p.m. bedtime all the year round, boys naturally did not go to sleep straightaway, particularly when the age range was from seven to fourteen. 'You went to bed at night at 7.30 and you listened to the Cathedral bells, and you cried yourself to sleep, or the bells put you to sleep.' Dormitory rules were strict and prefects were appointed to keep order, but (in 1905), 'There were frequent pillow-fights and chariot races, one dormitory challenging another. For the chariot races, four boys – two boys at the front and two at the rear – would pull another boy on a blanket along the polished floor. One boy was posted as sentry. Execution by hanging was then the custom and sometimes took place at Strangeways Gaol whose tower could be seen from one of the dormitory windows. It was always at 8.00 p.m. We had heard that someone was to be hanged, so on that particular day, as soon as the teacher on duty had departed, as many boys as possible crowded round

the window, picturing in our minds the scene in the con-
demned cell and on the gallows. It was only afterwards that
we discovered that the poor chap had been hanged at 8.00
a.m., twelve hours earlier than our rather eerie and macabre
vigil.'

Should the boys not be in their beds, or should there be any
noise, punishment was severe if the House Governor was on
one of his fairly regular prowls. It was on such an occasion in
the late 1920s that the following incident occurred. The dormitory was L-shaped with stairs leading up to the short area,
and a boy was quietly playing a ukelele in his bed at the far
end. Boys nearest the stairs guessed that Governor Fielden was
listening and waiting on the stairs. They stopped talking and
the silence spread through the rest of the dormitory until only
the tinkle of the ukelele could be heard. The player then
realised something was wrong. 'Why have you all gone quiet?'
he asked. This is what followed.

The Governor stormed in. 'Right!' he said, 'all of you out of bed.'
He went into the middle dormitory. 'Out of bed.' He went into the
small dormitory. 'Out of bed. Stand at the bottom of your bed.
Turn. Downstairs you go.' We were in our nighties, like long white
cricket shirts. 'Stand up on your lockers. Face the wall. Now, listen.
Beds are provided for you to sleep in. You have clean linen every
week. You have very clean dormitories. There are thousands of
children not only throughout the world but in this country who
would willingly change places with you. But you apparently don't
appreciate it. You take it for granted. We can't do enough for you.
If Humphrey Chetham could see you now he would immediately
say: 'Be damned with the bequest.' This is Chetham's Hospital,
caring for those in need, and you are supposed to be in need. And
how are you responding? Sometimes, I'm disheartened.' He nearly
made us cry. 'All right. You don't like bed. You can stand here all
night and I'll bet tomorrow night you'll enjoy your bed. I might
come back, but on the other hand I might not. If I do come back
and find that anybody has got down, they will incur my wrath.'
Half-past eight came, half-past nine and half-past ten. Nobody
said a word. We daren't, because we knew he would come creeping
in again. We stood on our boxes with our faces to the wall. It's
most monotonous to stand facing a painted wall, in your nightie,
on a locker and the light fading. After a long time he returned.
'Right! Stand down. I've relented. We want you to be of some use

tomorrow. Starting with the youngest, off to bed you go. When you get back think how nice it is to have a nice bed to return to. In future, watch it!' We went back to bed, all ninety seven of us. Nobody coughed, nobody sneezed, there wasn't a sound.

Fifty years later, details of this kind are still being clearly remembered, not only in this instance but in many others where the discipline of the school was being enforced. Caning was a normal punishment and canes were kept in a locked cupboard in the cloisters. 'He would ceremoniously undo it, select a particular cane and sharpen the end with a very sharp penknife. He used to sharpen it to a point, I think it was to stop it splitting. He would perform a few swishes through the air, and his prelude was nearly as bad as his punishment. You had to stand with your hand out, and instead of him moving to the other hand, you had to step aside to bring your other hand in line with the cane. You shuffled backwards and forwards like that until you had your ration of six strokes. I never remember being given less than six' (1920).

Chetham's was not exceptional in allowing corporal punishment as the cane and the strap were in general use in other schools, but there were times when punishment might have been too freely administered. 'We were only babies – I was seven and a half – and we knew nothing else. We were fatherless boys, we couldn't run home to anybody. I was fairly good at school work so I was rarely in trouble, but I used to cringe sitting at the side of one poor boy who was no good at mental arithmetic and used to take some awful hidings. I wouldn't go so far as to say that because of what we went through I don't believe in corporal punishment where it is necessary, but he couldn't help being less bright than anyone else. It was wrong to beat him when he clearly had no conception of what was going on' (1926).

It was generally accepted that punishment was the risk undertaken when rules were broken, but it was also generally known that punishment would be given when undeserved, or even when the reason was unknown. 'The whole background was secluded and there was no justice. When you left you were still only a little boy, and you were frightened. Through the terror which surrounded me as I grew up, I was frightened myself. Your confidence goes. I've had to do everything to break down that barrier. I don't think sensitive children could take it. I like to think that I went there, but at the same time I live in terror thinking about what it was like while I was there' (1931).

A different kind of punishment was the 'march'. A boy could be put on the 'march' for a stated length of time during which he would be required to walk forwards and back along a path which was visible from the teacher's room. 'I got it once for all my spare time for a week, and it was my most miserable time. I don't know to this day what I had done to deserve it. You got punished for some unknown reason. Sometimes it depended on the temper of the master. I never got very much corporal punishment. I got the strap, but never the cane. But as for that week on the "march", it nearly broke my heart' (1915).

Although a strict discipline was maintained throughout the school, a questionable toughness characterised the ways in which the Senior Master and the House Governor imposed that discipline. Being tough could be regarded as appropriate training for the tough life that was expected after leaving school. 'I once very seriously damaged my hand. I was standing in the Day-room doorway, a gust of wind blew the door very hard, and before I could get my hand out, the thick, studded oak door closed quickly and banged my hand in the framework of the door. Governor Fielden came on the scene. I was crying, as a boy of eight would be with an injury like that. I was taken to Salford Royal Infirmary to have it bandaged up. I always remember him saying to me: "Chetham's boys don't cry", and I think that was the only time I can remember crying when I was at Chetham's. We had that spirit, we would put up with injustice.'

The tightness of the discipline met with a challenge when, after 1926, most of the senior boys were at other schools on weekdays. Their day would begin as usual at 6.00 a.m., but after trades and breakfast they would change into their civilian suits, line up for inspection and the issue of three halfpence for tramfare, and move quickly off. They would return for a hurried midday meal, dash back to their schools, and return for tea, homework and a later bedtime. In some cases a divided loyalty developed, and it was not easy to keep track on all that was going on. One boy, for example, was expelled for truancy after it was discovered that, although he left with other boys, he absented himself from lessons in his other school. Experiences of this nature led to a restriction in 1933 on the number of boys who were allowed to be educated elsewhere. Only boys who in the opinion of the House Governor could be relied on were permitted to leave the premises.

With this slight modification, the pattern at Chetham's remained virtually as it had been in the nineteenth century until the school was evacuated. 'I don't regret those eight years. In fact, those eight years are the finest years of my life and there was a lot of character-making among them, but for the cruelty of the staff. That's the only thing that worried me' (1934). 'Taken all round, I consider it rather a happy period. You felt that the restrictions, now you look back on them, although they were a bit onerous, they were for your own good. To me as a boy who was apt to go astray when I got in the school through my parents not being about, you wanted some actual control and you got it in the school. Most of the boys were prepared to accept the conditions, but we all counted the days, minutes and seconds when we should be leaving the school' (1915).

A happy period? Each day was regulated, punishments were severe, yet in retrospect there was a general appreciation for what was achieved. In addition there was always gratitude for the special occasions such as the School Camp, the Whitsuntide Walk, and the visit to Lord Egerton's Tatton Hall.

School Camp had come about in an unusual way. In 1870, one of the boys, William Entwistle, left the Hospital and twenty-eight years later sent in a gift of £5 'by way of a thank offering' when he learned that there was a deficiency of income. The next year, 1899, he sent another £5, and also £1 5s 0d 'to provide a threepenny piece to be given to each boy on his leaving for the holidays'. From his own experience he knew of the impoverishment of families. Then in 1902 he sent in £20 saying that £5 should be given to school expenses as in previous years, but that the £15 balance should start 'a Boys' Holiday Fund with the view of sending the Chetham Boys occasionally to the seaside'. He himself had never had a holiday at the seaside while he was in the Hospital. The intention was so novel, particularly coming from a former 'poor boy', that he was invited to attend a Governors' meeting to explain what the scheme would entail. He felt too unequal to attend such a meeting but set out his ideas in a letter. 'I am a believer in boxes because they make it possible for systematic giving, and a boy or man can spare weekly what he cannot, or does not, manage to give in a lump.' Fund raising began. By 1904, all the boys had a day trip to the seaside. By 1913, there was sufficient collected for the whole school to be transported to the seaside for a fortnight. Although there were no Summer Camps during World War I they were resumed in the post-war years, and regular Camp Fund concerts took place with visiting artistes to swell the funds. The practice continued after World War II with the Free Trade Hall becoming fully booked by supporters, only by then it was the school, and not visiting artistes, who provided the entertainment. Much of the reputation gained locally by the school for musical performance stemmed from these Camp Fund concerts. An idea that had begun with boxes had blossomed into a very valuable support for the school. It was intended, as William Entwistle wrote in his letter to the Governors in 1902, 'as a thank offering for blessings and mercies received in the past'.

Camp concerts took place on an improvised stage in the schoolroom.

> The floor was rough and ready. I can remember some young ladies coming ballet dancing, and they went off crying because the floor was just planks of wood and it was very uneven and they couldn't manage. The following year they got some very thick plywood which made a very nice floor so that they could carry on. We enjoyed singing at Camp Concerts. We would spend a lot of time after school rehearsing and there was nothing I enjoyed more than getting on the stage and singing: 'My Grandfather's clock, tick tock', heads going from side to side. Parents and old boys used to enjoy it too.

Camp itself was a highlight of the year. 'It seemed to be the one time when everything was free and easy. The discipline was still there but it wasn't irksome. We didn't have to get up in a morning and sweep a schoolroom out or whatever you did for a trade. By today's standards the camp was probably too elaborate because the whole domestic staff attended as well as the teachers, so we had a big dining-room marquee with wooden tables, which was equivalent to the Baronial Hall. Of course, the food was the same as we would have at school, prepared by the same people. We had coach trips, mountain walks, days by the sea, swimming in the sea and visits to places of interest. All these were beyond the means of our families.'

Even in such idyllic surroundings there could be a reminder of the need to observe accepted rules. 'I had just pulled this girl out of the water. She was in difficulties and was drowning, mind you, so I pulled her out. I had just got her to the side, when the master on duty called my name. 'Yes, sir,' I replied. 'Come here', which I did and he gave me a clout. Now this child's father saw him and said: 'What are you clouting that little lad for?' 'Well,' he said, 'he's not supposed to play with the public.' 'Why not? Why shouldn't he?' came from the father, 'He's just saved my daughter's life!' (1933).

Every Whit Monday the uniformed Chetham's boys led the procession of between two and three thousand Sunday School scholars and teachers from the Church of England schools in Manchester. 'We were practising for weeks and weeks before marching. We used to be in three groups, about thirty boys in each, with three banners. We were used to marching in step but there is a difference in doing two abreast and four abreast across wide streets and round corners. I reckon we were nearly as good as the Guards as we walked through Manchester. I can remember old ladies in the streets saying: 'Eee, aren't they bonny, aren't they lovely!' because we had our yellow stockings and flat caps.'

School uniform was not worn for the visit to Tatton Hall, the home of Lord Egerton, one of the feoffees. 'We had been hearing rumours about the proposed trip all week and on the day we were told we weren't to go to school in the afternoon, but we were to go the the wardrobe and take out what we called 'camp dress', which was grey shorts instead of blue, and grey shirts. Two coaches arrived, I think they were called charabancs in those days. We were shown the Park, the Chinese garden, the lake and I remember having a trip round the lake in a genuine Indian birchbark and a dugout canoe. We were even allowed to have rides on the motor cars.'

Another memory: 'Believe me, one year Lord Egerton said: "Do you want a ride, William, in this car?" I said, "Yes. sir", though how he knew I was called William I don't know. It was M1, the first car that was built in Cheshire, and I had a ride in that year, with the old Lord driving.'

On such occasions there are usually moments of amusing embarrassment. 'This certain day we were at Lord Egerton's and all the lads were swimming in his lake. All of a sudden, Miss Judith and Miss Clarke appeared – that was Dr Clarke's daughter and Judith is the House Governor's daughter. As soon as the lads saw Miss Judith coming, they all dived into the blooming lake or under the seats of the ornamental summer house. They weren't wearing costumes and were as naked as the day they were born, and some of them were big lads, you know, not little ones.'

Perhaps it would seem appropriate to conclude this section with the words from the oldest surviving pupil of the school, whose eyes still sparkle as he recalls the years 1898 to 1905 when he was at Chetham's. There was a band in those days and he was playing the euphonium when his time came to leave at the age of fourteen. 'The Bandmaster advised my mother to let me take up a musical career for which he said I had the potential. But there were no such things as musical scholarships in those days, and as we were very poor (my father having died when I was four years old, leaving my mother with four children to bring up), I had to find a job to earn some money, which I did – office boy at a firm of solicitors at four shillings a week. I am now a happy and contented nonagenarian, having discovered that happiness is less dependent on the accident of circumstances than is generally supposed, and is more a matter of direction, choice and habit. As for Chetham's, the discipline was strict but salutory, and it stood me in good stead throughout my long life, and especially during my four years in the army in the 1914-1918 war.'

The Warden's room of 1421 which became the Library Reading Room in 1656

The 'Baronial Hall': the original college refectory, then the school dining hall until 1978: now a chamber concert hall.

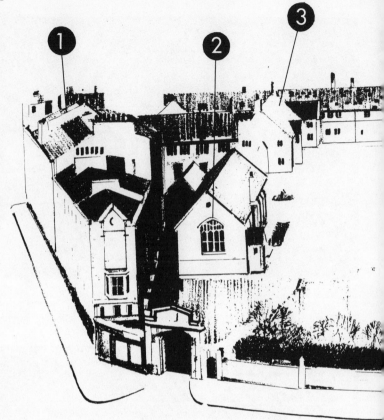

The school site today

(1) Palatine House
(2) The Schoolroom
(3) Library
(4) Original college building
(5) Long Millgate College building
(6) Classroom block

Right   The school from the air, before the recent acquisitions

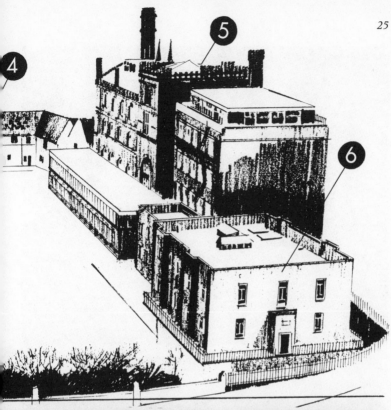

Tossing the pancake in the old kitchen, about 1910

In the workshop set up in 1888

Ablutions: morning washing; numbered toothbrushes

Midday meal, 1956

In the Snug Dormitory 1956: now the School Library

CHAPTER 2

Education at the Hospital School

Most children of poor parents in the seventeenth century had
no formal education. A few might be chosen for the free grammar schools where Latin and Greek were taught in preparation
for a career in law or the Church, or a few might be chosen for
hospital schools such as Chetham's, in preparation for apprenticeship.[1] There is evidence that in the eighteenth century boys
had been put to work while still at school, but with the
nineteenth century, education at Chetham's had become form-
alised, as is illustrated in the timetable shown opposite.

The terminology is indicative of a utilitarian approach to
education. There is the 'general routine of daily instruction',
and the detail shows how the children were 'employed', rather
than having their abilities fostered. There would be no school
teaching on Thursday or Saturday afternoons, but as the boys
were not allowed outside the walls of the institution without
permission, there was little opportunity for leisure activity.
There were two teachers, with assistants, and the House
Governor was responsible for general welfare. The number of
boys had increased to one hundred, the Hospital was run
according to strict rules, and Chetham's was to retain this
purposeful structure until the middle of the twentieth century.

A possibility for change had arisen in the 1870s and the
reasons why no change took place throw an important light
on why Chetham's was to retain its formal structure into the
twentieth century. A request was made to the Charity Commissioners for the number of boys to be increased to one
hundred and fifty and for a new schoolroom to be built. This

1 How many and where, such schools were being founded is a matter of
conjecture. In 1667, the Old Swinford Hospital was founded by Thomas
Foley for children of poor, honest parents of the craftworker and labouring
classes under terms similar to those at Chetham's. The Assistant County
Archivist of Hereford and Worcester has reported that a copy of Humphrey
Chetham's will has been discovered in records relating to the foundation,
and the parallel is so close that it can be assumed that the Swinford Hospital
was based on the Chetham's model.

GENERAL ROUTINE

OF

DAILY INSTRUCTION IN THE SCHOOL OF CHETHAM'S HOSPITAL,

ON

MONDAYS, TUESDAYS, WEDNESDAYS, AND FRIDAYS.

MORNING.

TIME	FIRST CLASS: HOW EMPLOYED.	DAY	TIME	SECOND CLASS: HOW EMPLOYED.	DAY	TIME	THIRD CLASS: HOW EMPLOYED.	DAY
8½—9½	PRAYER READ	*Daily*	... ...	... ...	... ...	... ...	... ...	... ...
— —	ENGLISH GRAMMAR	*Monday*	To 9¾	READING, ENGLISH HISTORY	*Monday*	— 9½	WRITING	*Monday*
— —	CHRONOLOGY and HISTORY	*Tuesday*		" 4th BOOK	*Tuesday*		ENGLISH HISTORY	*Tuesday*
— —	PROPHECIES, &c.	*Wednes.*		" ENGLISH HISTORY	*Wednes.*		WRITING	*Wednes.*
— —	CHURCH CATECHISM	*Friday*		" 4th BOOK	*Friday*		CHURCH CATECHISM	*Friday*
9½-10½	WRITING	*Daily*	9¾—10½	" ENGLISH GRAMMR.	*Monday*	9½—10½	READING, 4th BOOK	*Monday*
				" SCRIPTURE HISTY.	*Tuesday*		" 3rd BOOK	*Tuesday*
				" ENGLISH GRAMMR.	*Wednes.*		" 4th BOOK	*Wednes.*
				" SCRIPTURE HISTY.	*Friday*		" 3rd BOOK	*Friday*
	INTERVAL.			INTERVAL.			INTERVAL.	
10—11	SPELLING	*Daily*	— 11	SPELLING	*Daily*	— 11	SPELLING	*Daily*
11—12	READING, ENGLISH HISTORY	*Monday*	11—12	ARITHMETIC	*Daily*	11—12	ARITHMETIC	*Daily*
	" JEWISH DO. ..	*Tuesday*						
	" 4th BOOK	*Wednes.*						
	" GEOGRAPHY ...	*Friday.*						
	AFTERNOON.			**AFTERNOON.**			**AFTERNOON.**	
2 —2¾	READING, SCRIPTURE LESSNS.	*Daily*	2 —2¼	WRITING	*Daily*	2 —2¾	WRITING	*Daily*
2¾—3½	WRITING FROM MEMORY ...	*Daily*	2¾—3½	SCRIPTURE LESSONS	*Daily*	2¾—3½	SCRIPTURE LESSONS	*Daily*
	INTERVAL.			INTERVAL.			INTERVAL.	
— 4	MENTAL ARITH. OR TABLES	*Daily*	— 4	MENTAL ARITH. OR TABLES	*Daily*	— 4	MENTAL ARITH. OR TABLES	*Daily*
4—5	ARITHMETIC ON SLATES ...	*Daily*	4 —5	ARITHMETIC ON SLATES ...	*Daily*	4 —5	ARITHMETIC ON SLATES ...	*Daily*

MORNINGS OF THURSDAYS AND SATURDAYS.

TIME	FIRST CLASS: HOW EMPLOYED.	TIME	SECOND & THIRD CLASSES: HOW EMPLOYED.
8½ — 9½	ARITHMETIC	8½ — 9½	ARITHMETIC ... ...
9½ —10½	READING BIBLE	9 —10½	READING BIBLE ... ...
	INTERVAL.		INTERVAL.
— 11	CHURCH CATECHISM	— 11	CHURCH CATECHISM ... ...
11 — 12	LEARNING EXPLANATION OF CATECHISM ...	11 — 12	LEARNING EXPLANATION OF CATECHISM ...

was at a time when Board schools were being built to meet the terms agreed in the 1870 Education Act for the education of the poor. The Charity Commissioners explained that they could not give approval 'until the consent of the Endowed Schools Commissioners had been obtained'. Under Section 55 of the Endowed Schools Act 1869, the whole question of the merits or otherwise of hospital schools was being examined, and an Assistant Commissioner was sent 'to confer with the Governors on the subject of their application and generally on the future constitution and management of the Foundation'.

The delay was unexpected because the governor had assumed that approval would be automatic, and they had commissioned Alfred Waterhouse, the architect responsible for Manchester Town Hall, to produce a plan for the new schoolroom. What was more disturbing was the refusal of the Commissioners 'to approve of the maintenance of Chetham's Hospital simply on its present footing, still less can they authorise its enlargement without some substantial change in its constitution'. Change, it was argued, was necessary 'to bring the Foundation more into harmony with the altered conditions of society'. The benefits of the Hospital 'are not so obvious in the present day as at the time when Humphrey Chetham founded his Institution. It was more necessary then than now to take a boy from the squalor and hardships and isolation of his home and submit him to regular discipline and constant supervision. Nowadays the majority of boys can get good elementary education at very little cost close to their own house.'

According to this report, there was no longer any need for a Hospital School. National day schools were now being made available, and although elementary education was not yet free, it was argued that the cost to families was small. 'Certainly if it is worth while taking a number of boys from their homes and providing them with maintenance so as to spare all cost and responsibility to their friends, it is worth while to give them more mental culture and training than could be obtained for them at home by an expenditure of 2d a week.' Chetham's would have to change into a more advanced school where boys would receive 'more mental culture and training' than in a national day school. There were precedents for modernizing hospital schools, and the report mentioned decisions which had recently been made in respect of Emanuel Hospital, London and Colston's Hospital, Bristol.

It was speculated that Chetham's might become a technically biased school with an admission age not below eleven or twelve. There should be no increase on the hundred boys then at the school, and 'admissions should be made dependent on merit tested in some suitable and satisfactory way'. The instruction should be in certain branches of practical science and science applied to the arts, and opportunities given to scholars to see processes in various Manchester workshops. An alternative was suggested should this type of reorganisation not be practical. Chetham's could be divided into two sections, a junior grade for forty boys aged ten to fourteen providing education of the standard elementary type, and a senior grade for sixty boys aged fourteen to sixteen who would undertake more technical work. These proposals reflect the demand for a more skilled labour force. Chetham's would cease to be a charity school and would become a more specialist school, with selection based on merit and not on social need. The entry age and the leaving age would be raised. The case for change was based on the assumption that Chetham's had outlived its usefulness in the altered world of 1873.

A final decision was not to be reached until three years later. Possibly the change of government in 1874 may have contributed to the abandonment of the proposals. Education had become very much entangled with inter-church rivalries, with Liberal Nonconformists opposing Tory Anglican groupings. In 1874 the Liberals were out, and the Tories were in. A delegation of nine went to London to meet with the Commissioners, and of the nine, five were members of Parliament.[2] 'The Commissioners on learning from the deputation that the Governors did not wish for any new scheme, stated that they would abandon the idea of preparing a new scheme for the Chetham Charity until they heard from the Governors that they wished to have one.'

The main objection to the proposals was the different method of entry into the school. 'The Governors have frequently observed with the deepest interest and sympathy the self-denial and hard struggle of a widowed mother, and in the case of orphans the praiseworthy efforts of a brother or a sister or more distant relative of friend of the family, to maintain a bereaved child in his early years in the hope of his becoming a future recipient of Humphrey Chetham's bounty. The Governors are apprehensive if the Educational Standard of admission be placed too high and the age of admission too old, that the gates of the institution will be closed against many of the 'Honest, industrious and painful Parents' whom Humphrey Chetham proposed to favour.'

2 The Hon Wilbraham Egerton, MP; the Hon Algernon Egerton, MP; S. W. Clowes, MP; T. W. Tatton; Hugh Birley, MP; Edwin Hardcastle, MP; Rev H. M. Birch; Oliver Heywood; R. Milne Redhead.

As for the development of scientific and technical skills at the school, the Governors submitted that the surplus income from revenue which had led to the original request for a new schoolroom was 'altogether insufficient for any such larger extension of the benefits of the Endowment'. They added that they were 'not in favour of the extension of Chetham's endowment to girls', a proposal which had been put forward by the Commissioners. The school should remain as it was. 'The Governors trust that amid the many educational Establishments, systems and experiments of the present day, the Chetham Foundation may be maintained in its integrity and independence with undiminished powers to confer its exceptional benefits, and that the same system of administration may continue which has provided for many generations, and which can claim on its behalf the approval of the test of time.'

The new schoolroom, designed by Alfred Waterhouse, was officially opened on 27 April 1878. The building, according to the *Guardian, Manchester* was 'in the Tudor style of architecture and harmonises well with the adjoining fabric'. Even today it looks like a chapel linked with the College buildings and is often mistaken for one, but its purpose was to provide more teaching space. Inspectors were to draw attention to its shortcomings as a classroom: 'On cold winter days it is impossible to sufficiently warm the large, handsome and airy main room by the open fire-places' (1901). 'The rooms are cruelly cold' (1906). Glass partitions were introduced, but the heating was still inadequate 'despite the erection of two large stoves in place of the open fire-places. It appears impossible to heat sufficiently such high pitched rooms without the introduction of hot water or steam pipes with radiators along the walls remote from the stoves' (1907). Classes were still being taught there until 1955 when the grammar school buildings became available. The building was then put to different purposes to meet the needs of the school, notably the division horizontally of the tall room to provide an orchestral practice room.

At the official opening, speeches were made throwing light on the discussions that had been taking place about the siting of the schoolroom. There had been talk of moving the school away from the centre of an industrialised city. The Dean of

Manchester 'sincerely hoped that the college would not be moved away to the country as some persons strongly advocated. It would be a great loss to Manchester to lose, with the exception of the Cathedral, the only bit of genuine antiquity which it possessed. Mills and warehouses could be seen elsewhere, but nowhere else could they see so fine an object of antiquity as Chetham's Hospital.' He thought that group of buildings ought not to be removed merely for the sake of the value of the ground. Edwin Hardcastle, MP, said 'he was very glad that the railway station, which the Dean feared might be built on the site of the college, was to be erected on the other side of the river'. The river is the river Irwell, and in 1884 Exchange Station was opened on the opposite side from Chetham's.

In 1876 when approval was finally forthcoming from the Commissioners for Chetham's to continue as it always had done, there appeared the novel: *The Manchester Man* by Mrs G. Linnaeus Banks. The book has become indelibly linked with Chetham's because of the detailed and accurate description of how Chetham's was run at the beginning of the nineteenth century. Although Mrs Banks was writing some seventy years later, the fact that there would be no change at Chetham's gave credence to her story. There was considerable pride in Manchester and the surrounding districts for a school which had existed for over two centuries and which had trained over three thousand boys. She gave a realistic assessment of the school's purpose:

> The training and education of the Chetham College boys was, and is, conducted on principles best adapted for boys expected to fight their way upwards in the world. They were not cumbered with a number of 'ologies' and 'isms'. . . their range of books and studies were limited. Reading, writing and arithmetic, sound and practical information, alone were imparted, so much as was needed to fit the dullest for an ordinary tradesman, and supply the persevering and intelligent with a fulcrum and a lever. Nor did their education end with their lessons in the schoolroom, nor was it drawn from books and slates alone.[3]

There is an underlying implication that anything beyond

3 Mrs G. Linnaeus Banks, *The Manchester Man*, p. 53. (John Sherratt and Son Ltd., 1970).

learning basic skills would not be needed. Similar views, with a wider social relevance, were to be expressed in a Founder's Day sermon delivered by the Rev John Hanby, who had been a regular visiting examiner of religious teaching at the school. They may seem reactionary today, but are worth noting because of their relevance at the time and the fact that a pattern of thought was being expressed which was to characterize the school until the Blue Coat period ended in 1952. Too much learning could be dangerous for working-class children, and education should be limited to what was necessary to earn a living. Great stress was laid on obedience, and the development of the intellect was to be discouraged. The text was from Ecclesiasticus: 'Hast thou children? Instruct them and bow down their neck from their youth':

Much attention is being given in the present day to the improvement of education. The restless activity of the age has called forth many changes that are considered to be essential to fit the youth of this country for their work in life. Whether the present demand for a knowledge of so many additional subjects was really good for the future interests of children, and whether they would become really wiser and better for being taught so many things, it was open to grave question. . . In proportion as the system of instruction in schools had been extended, the duty of enforcing discipline seemed to have become a matter of secondary importance. Impatience of restraint, disregard of lawful authority, independence of action – even at an early age – now appears to characterize the rising generation, and particularly the children of what were commonly knows as the 'Working Classes'. . . The duty of obedience, the duty of respectful attention to the commands of authority, of respectful demeanour in the presence of superiors, of doing what was right because it was right, of a cheerful and ready submission to teachers and masters, was at Chetham's Hospital enforced in a degree which left nothing to the better part of the natures of these poor children, as they grew up. . . To remove the yoke, which a man should bear in his youth, was no kindness to children, and would not but result in trouble. . . Education must not be confounded with mere instruction. The tendency of the age was to confound the two, and indeed to regard the development of the intellectual powers as all they need strive after in the bringing up of children. On all accounts that was to be regretted; and it was to be hoped that the Institution might continue to be, as it always

had been, so far, one in which poor children might be really educated
– trained as to the faculties of their minds and souls, in conformity
with the teaching of the Church, in the first place; and, then, efficiently
instructed in useful knowledge that should fit them for their work in
the world.[4]

Grants were payable to schools whose pupils were successful
in examinations conducted by the Science and Art Department
of the Board of Trade. The Great Exhibition of 1851 had drawn
attention to the need for technical instruction, and the Department awarded grants to encourage science and art teaching
in schools. From 1881 such grants came to Chetham's for pupils
reaching the required standard. Grants were also payable in
respect of 'Manual' (woodwork), and in 1888 Mr W. Mather of
Salford Ironworks 'offered to fit up at his own expense Smiths'
and Joiners' workshops at the Hospital'. The House Governor
submitted a building plan for the workshops together with
proposals that 'the Technical shops might be worked without
increased cost to the Charity' by using the additional skilled
mechanic and joiner on maintenance and general repair work
in addition to instruction. The copper plate fixed to the wall
in the workshop in 1925 reads: 'This Workshop was built in
1888 and was equipped by The Rt Hon. Sir William Mather.
The workshop was enlarged and modern equipment installed
by Louis E. Mather, Esq.'
Additional financial support came with the Elementary
Education Act, 1891, which made it possible for a claim to be
made for state aid towards the cost of education at the Hospital. Previously only the new Board schools had been able to
make such a claim, and grants would be made in accordance
with a report by an inspector, the 'payments by results' system,
by which inspectors could determine the amount of the grant.
The standard at Chetham's was at least as good, if not better,
than the average elsewhere. In 1890 the inspector reported:
'Though this school does not claim a grant, the curriculum
prescribed by the Code has been strictly followed in both
elementary and class subjects, and includes French in the first
class. The instruction had been on intelligent lines throughout,
and the Boys are receiving a sound elementary education.'

4 Rev. John Henn, *Memoir of Richard Hanby* (1886).

French had been introduced by the House Governor at that time and was to be discontinued when he retired.

In 1899 the gross educational state grant for Chetham's was £150 14s 9d. The determining factor was average attendance, which was ninety-nine, and for each of the ninety-nine pupils there was payment according to a fixed scale. The Principle Grant was 14s, and additions were made for discipline and organisation (1s 6d), drawing (1s 9d), singing (1s), object lesson and English (2s), geography (2s). For additional subjects, further grants were payable based on the number of hours teaching in each subject. A claim was allowed for one hundred and sixty-eight hours' instruction in French and shorthand at 1s an hour, as well as sixty-eight hours of manual instruction at 7s a hour. If discipline and organisation had not been good, the rate would have been 1s per child instead of 1s 6d. If singing had been only ear and not by note, the rate would have been 6d, not 1s. Inspectors came to schools and asked children to sing any one of twelve songs learned by rote. The extra 6d per child was paid if there were evidence that music reading was being attempted. The 'payments by results' scheme disappeared under the 1902 Education Act.

Education, then, was to fit children for work, an approach which would accord with what Mrs Banks had expressed in *The Manchester Man*, and would also be in accord with the wishes of the Founder. Mrs Banks had also referred to the 'persevering and intelligent' boy who would be provided with 'a fulcrum and a lever'. How would the brighter pupil fair at Chetham's? Such children in Manchester were to be given opportunity to transfer from an elementary school to a central school or a grammar school, but until 1926 these opportunities were not available at Chetham's which remained an elementary school with a school leaving age of fourteen.

Applications for apprenticeships were beginning to require qualifications beyond those skills learned in an elementary school. 'In hindsight, I regret that we did not have a Public Relations Officer to whom one could talk freely about job opportunities. The Masters were held in veneration, but were hardly the type to invite confidence. Because of this, I had to wait until the end of the First World War (by which time I possessed a First Class Army Certificate of Education) before I could enter a Technical School' (1905). Another boy who left in 1920 has commented: 'I had finished the school course a year before I left. For the last twelve months I carried on with Art on my own. I had no particular instruction because there was no teacher equipped to teach Art.' When asked whether he regretted this state of affairs, the reply was: 'Not really! There was only one thing that mattered then, and it wasn't higher education. It was getting a job when you left at fourteen. Your mind concentrated on that.'

Where an apprenticeship was available, the going was still good. 'An apprenticeship was secured for me with Royce Ltd. of Trafford Park. When we left the College we were rigged out with two suits of clothes, one for weekday wear and the other for Sundays. Also two pairs of shoes to suit a similar purpose. A month or so after starting work in the Pattern Shop at Royce Ltd. my Mother was instructed to attend the Office. I was then Indentured as a bound apprentice for seven years as an Engineer Pattern Maker at a starting wage of twelve shillings a week. This was considered very good for those days. My brother was less fortunate when he left the College at Easter 1919, for no job was found for him. It was very difficult due to the large number of 'demobbed' men from the forces' (1917).

Leaving a school which had also been home became even more of a break when the Blue Coat uniform was replaced by a civilian suit: Boys were measured and the clothes ordered, but only on the day of leaving did the transformation take place. 'We took them up to bed with us the previous night, we hardly slept, and as soon as we got up in the morning we were into those new clothes. We were fitted out with two suits, two pairs of boots, two shirts, two vests, two pairs of socks, and two caps. Stiff cuffs had gone out by my time. Previously, boys had worn old-fashioned detachable cuffs. That was the outfit. We thought we were beginning to be somebody. I was beginning to be regarded as a mature citizen, an adult' (1920).

Leaving the Hospital in the inter-war years no doubt lacked the security which had come with the purchased apprenticeship of earlier years, but much was done to ensure that employment was possible. The local reputation of the school itself served as a recommendation. 'Three of us went to a firm of solicitors and they were asked to pick one of us. I didn't get that job, but I was picked out of the three in the next one. I learned afterwards that the firm had made overtures to the school which had a reputation in the city. We were favourably received wherever we went. If we had no other attributes, at least we were respectful and well-mannered. That is a tradition which has always been accepted, that if you were a Chetham's boy, you were different from the others' (1926).

It was not always as easy to obtain employment. In one instance letters of application were written to a number of banks without any response, and in later years a possible ex-planation was given to the unsuccessful candidate by a retired bank manager: 'It doesn't obtain now, but it did at the time you left school. You had no father, that is why you were at Chetham's, you were living in straightened circumstances. Handling a lot of money would have been a great temptation, it was thought, however good your character may have been. We wouldn't take you on to save your character' (1931).

The days of election and indenture were drawing to a close. For nearly three hundred years the Hospital School had pro-vided for the welfare and the later employment of the boys entrusted to its care, but for some time a financial problem had been occupying the attention of the governors. In 1898 the House Governor had drawn attention to 'a decrease of income and an increase of salaries' in claiming an aid grant from the Manchester Diocesan Association of Church Schools, and added: 'Owing to the Agricultural depression it is possible that the income will be less this year, and our position is one of chronic poverty.' Rents from the college estates were lower, while educational expenditure was rising and there was always the main burden of feeding and clothing the boys. Expenditure could be cut by reducing the number of boys on the establishment, but the governors were reluctant to take so drastic a measure in 1898. Instead, each volunteered to make an annual contribution, and some stock was sold to liquidate debts that had accumulated. It was also decided to charge 6*d* to visitors for a conducted tour of the Library, which made an important contribution to school funds.[5]

5 See Appendix 3: *Visitors*.

These makeshift measures did not last long. In 1908 the number of boys had to be reduced from a hundred to seventy five. Public support rallied round the Extra Endowment Fund organised by the Old Boys' Association, which had been formed in 1878 when the new school room was opened, and by 1911 the number was back to ninety-nine, but only because the public appeal had met with such a strong response. The question still had to be faced as to whether the original source of revenue from investment on land, since re-invested, would be able to meet increasing educational costs and inflation brought about by World War I. It was found to be necessary that no boys be elected in 1916 because 'of the extra cost of maintenance caused by the war, and the loss on the last years' working as shown on the accounts'. In 1917 a notice appeared near the entrance to the Hospital telling visitors that the Institution was in need of financial assistance. In 1918 the number of boys had to be limited to seventy. A public appeal was again launched, and sufficient support was given to the Endowment Fund for the number of boys to reach ninety seven by 1929.

The cost of providing for all the needs of boys from families where there was extreme hardship left little reserve for extending the educational range within the school. Help came in 1926 when the opportunity was given for Chetham's boys to compete with other boys for scholarships to enter grammar and central schools. An inspection of the school had drawn attention to the fact that 'the boys are under a disability, as compared with the great majority of Manchester children, by being taught in classes containing two or more standards'. Chetham's was an elementary school with only two teachers who, in addition to resident duties, had to deal with a seven-year age range. The report also stated that, by comparison with other children, the boys had 'small opportunity for receiving advanced instruction in Secondary or Technical Schools'. The solution was for boys at the age of ten to sit for scholarships and free places at grammar, technical and central school. The cost of the education of successful boys would thus not be borne by the Endowment, which would concentrate its limited resources on welfare. An additional teacher was recruited to provide special preparation for the scholarship examination.

They were giving us a chance to compete with other boys in Manchester, a chance we never had before. We would have left school at the age of fourteen with no qualification other than having been at Chetham's. In other words, an employer would have assumed that you would do as you were told, that you were disciplined and probably honest, but that you were not likely to be as bright as a grammar school boy.

The scheme was so successful that by 1931, fifty-eight of the ninety-three boys at Chetham's were receiving their education outside Chetham's.[6] They were issued with a school uniform appropriate to the school they were attending and would wear their Blue Coat clothes only in the evenings and at weekends. Such boys would have an advantage over those who remained inside Chetham's. 'When I came out into the world when I was fourteen, I started serving a craft apprentice and I had to learn a different language. I used to call everybody "Sir" even though they were labourers. We didn't know what to expect in this different world. I had an inferiority complex, and so did other boys. We felt that the grammar school boys had an advantage over us. They had been out to other schools and were meeting other people, while we were behind four walls and weren't allowed out' (1938).

For the grammar school boys there would be school certificates recording examination success and they would not be leaving the Hospital until the age of sixteen or, exceptionally, eighteen. As for the others, the fourteen year old school leavers would have nothing. 'I applied for one job and they wanted a leaving certificate. I asked the House Governor for one and he said: 'We don't give leaving certificates,' and left it at that. The only proof I ever had that I went to Chetham's and left at the appropriate time was the certificate given to me by the Old Boys' Association' (1942).

An evening meal for boys over fourteen years of age was introduced for the first time, and the following rules were introduced. 'Supper to be served in the Dining Hall at 8 o'clock

6 Six at Manchester Grammar School; 17 at Central High School for Boys; 13 at North Manchester High School; 12 at Ducie Avenue Central School; 5 at Ardwick Central School; 1 at Hulme Grammar School; 1 at North Manchester Grammar School and 3 at Crumpsall Lane Council School.

on Monday, Tuesday, Wednesday and Thursday. Two orderlies to act as carriers. They should lay the tables and convey the food to the Dining Room, having everything ready before 8 o'clock. Boys to assemble punctually at 8 o'clock. They may leave the table immediately after they have finished, and return to their studies. Selected orderlies to be on Supper Duty for one week, and to be entirely responsible for the laying-up and clearing away of the meal. There will be *no* necessity to go to the kitchen and boys are strictly forbidden to do so.' No doubt they did occasionally, as there was always a warm relationship between the domestic staff and the boys and 'extras' would be slipped through the network of regulations. They would, however, be punished for this breaking of bounds.

New problems became evident when boys were regularly leaving the school premises each school day. One or two took it upon themselves to be absent from lessons at their other school. There were some adverse reports on lack of academic progress on some boys who had been successful in the qualifying examination and were at other schools. Also, some parents wanted their boys to earn money and contribute to the family budget at the age of fourteen even though an undertaking had been given that the boy would stay at grammar school until the summer term when he was sixteen. By 1933, it was decided that a limit should be placed on the number of boys attending outside schools. Only those who in the opinion of the House Governor would benefit from a secondary education were allowed to take the examination. The practice of allowing boys to go to central and technical schools was discontinued. Chetham's reverted to being a school for the seven to fourteen age group from which a grammar school contingent had been extracted, and that extract was closely monitored by the House Governor.

A great deal depended on the House Governor. Between 1874 and 1974 there were only four House Governors, which was an important contributory factor to the element of continuity within the establishment in spite of external change. In 1874 Richard Hanby, who had already served as Assistant Librarian in the Chetham's Library, became House Governor, responsible for the welfare and later employment of the boys and for the hiring of teachers to undertake teaching and resident duties. In 1886 he was followed by Walter Thurlow Browne who had been Master of the Boys' Refuge and House, Strangeways, Manchester. His wife became Matron and it was unprecedented for a House Governor and family to be quartered inside the Hospital. At first their young daughter was allowed to reside with them on payment of £20 per annum, a payment which was discontinued two years later. In 1912 William James Fielden, who had been an Assistant Teacher at Chetham's from 1901 to 1903, was appointed House Governor until he retired in 1948 at the age of sixty-eight. The last nine years were particularly demanding because of the dislocation caused by war and evacuation.

His successor was Harry Vickers, a former Chetham's boy who had been elected in 1926. In that year Easter Monday was on 5 April and the governors had decided to hold the election meeting on the next day, which happened to be the tenth birthday of Harry Vickers. Under the terms of the will, he would not have been eligible for election because he would already be ten years old on election day. There is a handwritten note on his petition to be considered for admission to the school: 'Although this boy will be over ten years of age on the day of election, had the latter been held on the usual day, viz. Easter Monday, 5 April, he would have been within the age limit'. Due notice was taken of this note, the petition was not excluded on age grounds, and he was elected. It is astonishing that someone who was to play so major a part in the development of the school could so nearly have been refused entry.

If Harry Vickers had been elected before 1926 he would have had to leave the Hospital on reaching the age of fourteen, but he was among the first group of Chetham's boys to be able to have a grammar school education. He attended the Central High School for Boys where he became Head Boy at the age of seventeen. Special permission was given for him to remain at the Hospital to qualify for a university scholarship. His widowed mother was not earning enough to maintain him, so the Hospital continued with support until he was awarded a City scholarship tenable at Manchester University. While he was at university, help continued to be given, which included the payment of graduation fees when he graduated with first class Honours. A further grant was made while he was taking a Diploma course to qualify as a teacher. There could not be a better example of the way in which Humphrey Chetham's endowment was being put to use in the changing educational climate of the 1930s. He became House Governor on 1 January 1949, and when he retired in 1974 he had successfully steered the school through two major reorganisations.

CHAPTER 3

The war years

Evacuation in August 1939 was to prove a watershed. After the buildings were damaged it was assumed that the boys would never return. For one boy it was the end of the old system: 'All the cobwebs of our closed, institutional world having been brushed away by the liberating evacuation to the Fylde coast, things could never be the same'.

Boys who had been conditioned to a strict régime in cloistered surroundings were translated to an environment which was difficult either to control or foresee. Administration was formidable because the responsibility of the feoffees for their care, maintenance and education had to be borne at a distance, and amid all the dislocation produced by the war. Only partial schooling was practicable and the difficulties that arose over billeting led to seeking the alternative of housing the boys under one roof in Derbyshire in 1943.

Administration was further complicated because there were two categories requiring differing treatment: boys who were still being educated at Chetham's and who were in billets in Cleveleys, and those attending outside schools who were evacuated elsewhere, although still under the overall responsibility of the governors. In January 1940 when the other schools returned to Manchester, accommodation had to be found for the thirteen boys attending those schools. The House Governor, who had served since 1912 and was already in his sixties, had to improvise as best he could, and conditions became more difficult with the call-up of teaching staff.

News of the blitz filtered through to the boys. 'The gentleman that we lived with was too old for National Service but he was in the Auxiliary Fire Service and was seconded to Manchester when the blitz was on. He had made it his business to go to the College to see the damage. He didn't know the names of the parts of the building, but he did drawings for us and we were able to fill in the gaps as to what he had seen. I was told afterwards that the feoffees were physically carting treasures out of the building and loading them into vehicles and taking them where they were safe from future bombings.'

The official report stated that the blast from a land mine which exploded outside the east end of Manchester Cathedral shattered the glass in almost every window in the Hospital, and the roof timbers were set on fire by incendiary bombs in several places. On the following night, 23 December 1940, more incendiary bombs were dropped causing further damage particularly to that part of the Hospital where the House Governors' private rooms were situated. His quarters and the contents became a total loss, and damage was also inflicted on the roof of the main hall and workshop.

'On Tuesday 24 December when help was practically unobtainable, Lord Egerton of Tatton (a feoffee) very kindly supplied a demolition party composed of his Estate men. As a result of their efforts the fire in the House Governor's quarters was finally extinguished. Lord Egerton also undertook to house most of the Hospital's valuable furniture at Tatton Hall, Knutsford, and fifty-one pieces had been that day taken to Tatton Hall by transport provided by Lord Egerton.'

Meanwhile the boys were discovering a different world in Cleveleys. 'We were the odd ones out because we were wearing a Tudor uniform in a modern seaside town.' Billeting varied, some being lucky while others had to sleep under the stairs so that bedrooms could be used by soldiers and airmen. There was no school for the first few weeks, until it was arranged for a shift system to operate, whereby Chetham's could use part of the local primary school for five mornings a week from 8.00 a.m. until 11.00.

> We had no money other than what we could earn by doing odd jobs for people. I remember at one period I used to go on a Saturday afternoon, at about five o'clock, to light the fire for a Jewish family. They must have been very orthodox, but the gentleman of the house stopped me in the street. He gave me a shilling each time because he said he knew I was a Chetham's boy and would not have any inhibitions about lighting a fire on a Saturday afternoon. Another thing we used to do was lay night lines on the beach to catch fish and then having given the landlady the pick of the catch, we used to sell the rest to the chip shop.

It was not possible to continue with woodwork lessons because wood was not available. Shoes, however, needed constant repairing. 'We had about eighty pairs because we had two pairs each, so the woodwork teacher taught us to mend shoes. We had two lasts and two benches. When there was a class going down in the main part of the school, there would always be someone hammering away at a piece of leather mending shoes.'

In 1943 the boys were moved into Bank Hall, Chapel-en-le-Frith, where they were all under one roof. The total of the school roll was fifty-four but the thirteen boys attending outside schools were transferred from Blackpool Grammar School to Buxton College where they stayed from Monday to Friday. 'We older boys from Blackpool Grammar were to be given special wartime accommodation in Buxton College which was a public school and very different. I was constantly in trouble for spending too much of my after-school time in Buxton (mainly in Buxton Library doing my homework and fancying myself as a really scholarly researcher) and not being nearly deferential enough once I finally arrived back at Bank Hall – for weekends of drills and parades, supervising the younger boys as a most reluctant prefect.'

The post-war policy of the hospital was under constant discussion. In November 1944, 'it was generally agreed that the Governors would not wish the boys to return and reside on Hospital premises'. The City Surveyor and the Cathedral authorities were consulted and plans for the redevelopment of the site were proposed. The buildings surrounding Chetham's were to be demolished[1] to create an island site with grassy lawns, the whole to become a religious and cultural centre with a Church House, a teaching centre for ordination candidates, a song school and a centre for religious drama. Possibly, societies such as the Manchester Literary and Philosophical Society, and Lancashire Parish Register and the Lancashire and Cheshire Antiquarian Society could be provided with a permanent centre and home. This dream depended on the non-return of the Chetham's boys, and sufficient money being available for demolition and reconstruction.

1. Manchester Grammar School, Corn Exchange, Palatine Hotel, Cathedral Hotel.

Manchester Cathedral Choir School was a separate institution, the only link being the permission granted yearly for
choristers to play football or cricket on the school yard for
limited periods. A similar provision was made for pupils from
Manchester Grammar School whose two buildings, con-
structed in 1870 and 1880, dominated Chetham's. The buildings were connected by a tunnel and a bridge which cut across
the entrance to Chetham's, and the feoffees were naturally very
sensitive about any encroachments on Chetham territory. The
Grammar School had no recreational space for their pupils,
who had to use city streets and school corridors in their break
and lunch times. Each year a formal request was made for a
junior form to be allowed to have a games period under supervision on Chetham's yard. The fact that there was no general
approval, but that the request had to be repeated annually,
may have produced this plea from the High Master in 1920:

> Dear Governor,
>   Year by year 'I come an humble suitor to your virtues'. May our
> Boys be allowed the same valued privilege as for so many years –
> two afternoons a week between hours of two and three? Will you
> put an humble petition to your Feoffees and tell them to see in Mr
> Harold Brighouse's last novel how much the boys appreciate their
> goodness.
>   Believe me,
>   Yours this year next year
>   sometime ever,
>   J. L. Paton.

The novel was *The Marbeck Inn*, in which a Grammar School
boy is depicted as 'staring gloomily out of the window at the
top of the stairs outside the Fifth Form room, watching the
boys of the Chetham's Hospital at play in that yard of theirs
which the Grammar School pretends to scorn but secretly
envies.'

There were twenty boys in the Choir School, with ten pro-
bationers, and all the boys were recruited and lived locally.
They were allowed on the yard between 1.00 and 2.00 p.m.
The choir sang Matins and Evensong daily, and the school was
housed near Victoria Station. Traditional dress of Eton suits
and mortar-boards with black tassels distinguished choristers

from the Blue Coat boys. In the early 1930s, extensions to the Cathedral made it possible for the Choir school to have a classroom and refectory on Cathedral premises. Choristers were evacuated in 1939 but the damage to the Cathedral in December 1940 placed the future of the Choir School at risk. It seemed natural that post-war planning would include provision of a place for choristers in Hospital buildings if the Chetham's boys were not coming back. Speculation was that Chetham's boys might be moved out of the centre of Manchester.

Rumours of such a change produced a howl of protest from the Old Boys' Association. 'Save the Blue Coat School' was a headline in the *Manchester Evening News* for 11 July 1945. The style of the article that followed echoed the special pleas of the 1870s, although this time the Governors were 'banishing' boys from Manchester and it was up to 'the people and merchants of Manchester' to stop them:

> After the strain of almost six years of war, and the consequent excitement of Victory in Europe, followed by the present General Election, it takes a special shock to bring the thoughts of the public round to matters that are occurring in their very midst. Yet the townsfolk. . . will learn. . . that the Chetham Hospital boys now evacuated to Bank Hall, Chapel-en-le-Frith, are not to return to residence. . . The banishment, and no other term fits the case, is the decision of the feoffees or governors due, we understand, to pressures by the Ministries of Health and Education. . . The people and merchants of Manchester and Lancashire have raised great sums for enterprises no less worthy than that of keeping the Blue Coat Boys in their midst.

An official explanation was forthcoming at the next meeting of the Old Boys' Association. It was explained that because of cramped accommodation and out-of-date sanitary conditions, the school would have to be moved elsewhere. Although Chetham's had turned out boys for a great number of years, the school was not equal to the requirements of modern education and health. The Hospital was no longer in a sufficiently strong financial position and could only provide for a small number of boys. Another complexity was the operation of the 1944 Education Act whereby schools were now classified into primary and secondary schools. Chetham's was neither, with its age range of seven to fourteen, which cut across the pattern of schooling which was being introduced. As for the buildings, it would not be practicable for repairs to be immediately carried out because government priority in 1945 was being given to domestic housing. These were the facts that had led to the possibility of the boys not returning to the centre of Manchester, but no decision had yet been made. Such was the position in 1945.

The years 1946-52 witnessed many meetings when the future of Chetham's was extensively examined. The decision was not one which the governors could unilaterally make, and a study of the relevant material shows that great care was taken to allow for all the hazards and hopes that characterised this period of educational development in England. It was not an easy decision to make, neither was it one which was certain to ensure an ultimate success. Many doubts, fears and hesitations had to be overcome and even when a point had been reached in 1950 when the grammar school solution was agreed, there followed a two year delay until the official sanction of the Ministry of Education could be published. The process began in July 1946, when representatives of the Ministry of Education met with the feoffees, the Dean of Manchester and members of the City Corporation. It was approved that the possibility of continuing the school in its existing premises should be considered, thereby reversing the decision made in the previous year that the boys would not be returning to the centre of the city.

The war was over, and at Chapel-en-le-Frith the boys were experiencing the mixed joys of a post-war austerity period. In 1945 the American Red Cross had provided two drums (40 lb) of dried milk and two boxes (20 lb each) of chocolate milk powder. A flying bomb had exploded at Combs Moss only ten minutes away from Bank Hall. In the severe winter of 1946-7 twenty five boys had worked on sleigh transport because the only communication with Bank Hall was by sleighs drawn by the boys across country. The Derbyshire War Agricultural Committee had relieved matters by delivering coal by caterpillar tractor. In other ways, conditions at Bank Hall were causing concern and in any event there was a five year lease on the Hall which would expire in 1948.

The long-term prospects of the school were still under examination, but it was decided that a start should be made by bringing the boys back. The number had to be limited to fifty and the same arrangements as had operated pre-war would, for the time being, be continued. There would be twenty-one boys under the age of eleven, twenty boys over the age of eleven in the Hospital School and nine attending outside secondary schools. Chetham's thus became a primary school to eleven plus, providing a secondary modern type of education for boys who did not gain places in outside grammar schools. Mention was made of choristers for the Cathedral, but the condition was laid down that they would not be available as choristers on week-days prior to 5.30 p.m. so that their ordinary education would not be interrupted.

A new House Governor/Headmaster would be needed, and there would be one or two resident Assistant Masters, a resident Matron, a Secretary and domestic staff. During the war only the Librarian had been daily at the Hospital, together with one of the domestic staff. The boys returned from evacuation on 17 April 1948. Mr and Mrs Harry Vickers took up duty as House Governor and Matron on 1 January 1949, replacing Mr W. J. Fielden, who had held the post for thirty-six and a half years and had been awarded an MBE, and his sister who had served as Matron after Mrs Fielden had died.

Wartime evacuation had undermined the discipline and corporate welfare which had characterised the pre-war school. It had not proved practicable in war time to exercise the same care and caution in the selection of boys as had been the tradition of election to Chetham's in the past. In consequence, some boys of an emotionally disturbed nature were in need of special care and attention which were beyond the resources of Chetham's. The first task of the new House Governor and Matron was to help such boys to overcome their difficulties. The first teacher to be appointed found himself, for example, dealing with a large number of senior boys who wet their beds each night. When appointed in March 1949, he had no expectation that Chetham's would become a grammar school. He recollects that the sending out of the more able boys to other schools was not satisfactory,

> And, in our rather idealistic view of Chetham's, it harmed the unity of the school. It was vaguely felt that one day we might not have to send boys out, that we would have a staff able to teach up to a high level, but it seemed to be assumed that we would always have boys who were there because they needed Chetham's, the children of poor but honest parents. To Harry Vickers, the intentions of the Founder were clear. He himself had been one who needed help, he had received it, and I think he intended to do what he could to see that when help was needed it would be given. A grammar school with its implication of a selection on a basis other than need was a different kettle of fish.

Yet by 1950 plans were being made for a change into a grammar school. The change was initiated by Harry Vickers. How could selection based on merit at the age of eleven-plus be reconciled with the Founder's intention that selection should be based on need within the seven to ten age range? In the 1870s, as we have seen, it was effectively argued that if the standard of admission were placed too high and the age of admission too old, 'the gates of the institution will be closed against many of the "honest, industrious and painful Parents" whom Humphrey Chetham proposed to favour'. In what ways were circumstances different in 1950?

The answer given was that the spirit of the Founder needed to be re-interpreted in the light of changes in society and in education. In the seventeenth century, indigence and need were the areas from which the boys had been selected from families whose respectability could be vouched for, and the boys would be provided with an apprenticeship. The intentions of the Founder related to a time when the poor had no educational opportunities, and when earning a living was by means of serving an apprenticeship. In the 1870s, there was still no free education available to the poor. By the middle of the twentieth century, not only had education been freely provided at the primary level, but free secondary education was now available under the 1944 Education Act. Children of poor parents now had opportunity to qualify for entry into the professions via further education, and apprenticeship schemes were being geared in some instances to academic success in graded examinations. In these changed circumstances, to deny a poor boy the possibility of taking advantage of enlarged educational opportunity would seem to run contrary to the intentions of the Founder. While it was regrettable that a change into a grammar school might possibly exclude from entry at the age of eleven-plus a boy who may have needed the support of such a school as Chetham's, social conditions had so changed that such a boy would not be as bereft as his equivalent would have been in the seventeenth century. The 'new poor' were in a better situation than the 'old poor', but they were still not in a position to benefit from new educational opportunities without help. The purpose of Chetham's was to help both kinds in the different educational structure.

While the possibility of change was being explored, the needs of the forty seven boys who had returned from Chapel-en-le-Frith were receiving full attention, although the two members of staff who had been at Bank Hall were no longer available. No boy now at the Hospital was a pre-war Chetham's boy. The sudden change from the open air and space of the countryside to the confined quarters at Chetham's was proving a great strain. The old spirit and tradition associated with the buildings, and which Harry Vickers himself had experienced and valued, had almost disappeared. Of the forty-seven boys, twelve were being educated at other schools and only thirty five were being educated inside Chetham's. There had been a marked reduction both in the number and quality of entrants into the school during the war years.

Before final proposals for reorganisation could be put forward, consultations were necessary with the city authorities, the Cathedral representatives and the Ministry of Education. The city authorities were in sympathy with the proposed change into a grammar school, but drew attention to the fact that so small a school would not be able to provide a sufficiently broad curriculum. If there was an expansion in numbers, planning permission for an additional building would be possible. Also, the possibility of amalgamating with Nicholls' Hospital School, another Manchester school which was also facing difficulties and a reduced school roll, was suggested.

The Cathedral representatives expressed interest in the possibility of choristers being educated at Chetham's, but no commitment was undertaken. It was the inclusion of music as a part of the reorganisation which interested the Ministry of Education.

The question of music, although incidental at this stage, had relevance to possible future support from local education authorities. It was thought unlikely that they would be willing to support an undifferentiated boarding school of small size in the middle of Manchester. Music would give an independent objective which could attract support, particularly as it would avoid class distinctions or any allegations that Chetham's was becoming a school for the privileged. Even so, there was no definitive plan as to what degree of musical education should be provided. What was being proposed in 1950 could well be too little for a musical school and too much for an ordinary school. Much would depend on how things developed. The intention in 1950 was that Chetham's would become not a school of music but a grammar school in which music would be an important part of the curriculum. The final scheme, which was to be published on 27 May 1952, contained this sentence dealing with entry after examination: 'Due attention shall be paid to the selection of boys possessing musical ability'.

Two further developments took place before Chetham's was officially recognised as a grammar school: the payment of fees, and the amalgamation with Nicholls' Hospital School. Chetham's was not in a financial position to provide for the needs of all the boys, or to undertake the expense of developing a grammar school. There would be scholarships, maintenance allowances and exhibitions payable within the resources of the Foundation, but otherwise fees would be needed to cover educational costs. In time, in addition to help from the Foundation, local authorities were to provide free places at the school. There also would be a junior school where fees would be payable, for the seven to eleven age group, which would make it possible for choristers to be available at the Cathedral. The introduction of fees and the establishment of a fee-paying junior school might give an impression that a fundamental change was taking place, but, at the time, the fees were minimal, care was taken for those in financial need, and fees were regarded as a means to one end: namely for Chetham's to continue in the old buildings fulfilling what was interpreted as the wishes of the Founder in the altered circumstances of the post-war period.

Nicholls' Hospital School had been founded in 1863 and was serving a similar purpose to Chetham's. There were two differences in that Nonconformist families could apply to Nicholls' whereas Chetham's had been restricted to Church of England membership, and that whereas selection for Chetham's had been restricted to five named parishes, a Nicholls boy could be selected from a five-mile radius of Manchester. Otherwise, conditions were similar. The age for election was the same, and similar attention as at Chetham's was paid to family background. The Hospital was situated in Hyde Road, Ardwick (away from the centre of Manchester) and had accommodation for a hundred boys. The number had declined to twenty two in 1945. In September 1939 the boys had been evacuated, but had moved back in March 1946. Declining revenues and increasing educational costs, as with Chetham's, were producing problems and the future of the Hospital would depend on the general educational policy of the City of Manchester with reference to the 1944 Education Act. It was at a meeting at the Town Hall that the possibility of amalgamation with Chetham's was broached by the city authorities, neither school having been consulted in advance.

Both schools were finding it impossible to continue on the same basis as before the war, and no major difficulties were to be experienced over amalgamation. It was agreed that in the matter of Foundation scholarships and maintenance allowances the beneficial areas should remain as previously – for Chetham's boys the five named parishes, for Nicholls' boys a five-mile radius from Manchester – but there was to be an extension to make provision for the education of boys 'belonging to Lancashire and Cheshire, and to the parts of Yorkshire and Derbyshire adjacent thereto'. In March 1950, twenty nine Nicholls boys arrived at Chetham's.

There was a natural rivalry between the two groups of boys

at first, with Nicholls' boys shouting 'Cheats' at the Chetham boys at football matches, but they soon settled down together. Within a few years they would be replaced by newcomers selected by examination. Until official approval from the Ministry of Education had been published, recruitment presented difficulties. The school was not yet a grammar school and, while newcomers were admitted for a grammar school curriculum, many of the Chetham's and Nicholls' Foundationers had not qualified for a grammar school education. At the end of 1951 the school roll showed a total of seventy six boys, with twenty one Chetham's Foundationers, seventeen Nicholls' Foundationers, nineteen new residents, five day seniors and fourteen day juniors. There were still eight senior pupils who were being educated in outside schools. Among the new entrants were eighteen boys who were already choristers before being admitted. The school was beginning to move in the direction of both academic and musical achievement.

The scheme made by the Minister of Education under the Charitable Trusts Act 1853-1925 was sealed on 27 May 1952. The general public, and in particular local education authorities, were now being informed about the nature of the changes that were taking place. 'The school shall be a day and boarding school for boys and shall be maintained in the present hospital buildings or in other suitable buildings, and its object shall be to give a Christian and liberal education. . . In framing the curriculum due regard shall be paid to the teaching of music, and arrangements may be made for boys to be members of church choirs and to sing therein.'

CHAPTER 4

The Grammar School

In 1945 a boy was elected to the Hospital School in the traditional way by means of a petition. His father had died in 1942, and his mother was left with three young children in war-time. He attended the local school but his mother was not satisfied with the education he was receiving. When she complained, she was told: 'What's the point of giving him more work to do? He can do the work easily. He will leave at fourteen to get into the mill to get money. Your family needs money, so what's the point of giving him extra work?' This answer was not acceptable to the mother. 'That isn't what I want for my child. I don't want him to live in the same squalor that we live in now. I want him to improve himself and get out of this.' A petition was submitted and the boy was accepted. He left home, to live not in the shattered buildings in Manchester, but in a large mansion in the Derbyshire hills.

Within weeks of joining he sat for the eleven-plus examination in accordance with the 1944 Education Act and became a grammar school pupil, travelling daily to Buxton College from Chapel-en-le-Frith. 'People thought I was from some sort of Borstal. They couldn't understand why I could be resident in one school, particularly one called a Hospital, and then going out for education.' It was not easy to match together the two elements of a grammar school approach to work and the strict attention to routine drills which were enforced at Bank Hall, Chapel-en-le-Frith. There were also disciplinary troubles in this confused period. The few Buxton scholars were allowed to keep their sweet coupons and buy sweets in Buxton, while the others had their sweets issued at weekends after a bulk purchase. 'We were always being bribed to get something from Buxton for the resident boys. On the train, bigger boys used to thrash us for our sixpences, or our sweet coupons, or for someone else's money. Ultimately, four boys got expelled for it.'

The boys returned to Manchester in the spring of 1948. 'We were pleased to return to Manchester. Although living in the country had its attractions, we were town boys. We were now nearer home, we could get visits from parents more easily; we could see human beings and shops instead of cows and fields. It was nice to get back into the old school building because we felt it was purposely built for us.' Oddly enough, although this was his first experience of the old building, the remark reinforces the feeling that Chetham's could only be associated with its fifteenth-century past. He was being educated at a city grammar school, but to all intents and purposed he remained a Chetham's boy.

As did Harry Vickers, also educated at a city grammar school, but who was appointed in January 1949 as House Governor to bring the school into the twentieth century while preserving those values which had characterised Chetham's. Both he and Audrey, his wife, devoted all their energies to make sure that the school would continue to fulfil the intentions of the Founder within the changed circumstances of the post-war world. For the next quarter of a century Chetham's was to be their life, and the survival of the school together with the high esteem which it receives at the present time, is due to their dedication. They began in war-damaged buildings, literally in a flooded bedroom, and they had to live with all the stresses and strains which accompanied the creation of a grammar school within a fifteenth century framework. Later, they were to pioneer the transformation of the boy's grammar school into a co-educational school for musically gifted pupils. No one could have foreseen in 1949 what lay ahead for Chetham's, except possibly Harry Vickers, whose purpose was to develop the potential of those entrusted to his care.

A sense of purpose was being restored. 'The difference when Harry Vickers took over was that we became civilised human beings. The discipline started coming from within the school itself. The boys became responsible for their own discipline, and the change was there immediately.' The batches of canes were burnt. 'I would be sent out on a Saturday afternoon to bring back boys who had run away.' Such was the experience of the last grammar school boy under the old scheme, as the new one was being introduced. He left for university and a professional career, and was fully aware of the changes that were taking place.

> The new entrants came from better homes and were selected because they were better than average. By then, lads from poor homes could be educated anywhere, and Chetham's was not needed in the same way that it had been needed fifty years before, or even in my time. I had needed Chetham's. Without Chetham's I would be nonentity. I like to feel that between my mother, myself and Chetham's, I've progressed and got myself out of what would have been a living death. The present school (1983) does not mean that much to me now, but the old school did. Bricks and mortar produce a nostalgia, though I just can't personally relate to the changes which have happened since I left.

There was widening educational opportunity in the post-war world and change at Chetham's was part of the general picture. Parents wanted their children to benefit from the new opportunities which were becoming available, and there was competition because of the population bulge. Even so, how could a school with no reputation itself as a grammar school, and housed in inadequate buildings, be attractive? Reasons would vary, but ultimately the test would be whether the arrangements being introduced would be satisfactory to parents. Previously, parents had been excluded from the school except for official visiting days and Camp Fund concerts. The school had taken over the child whose home was, for the time being, the school. Previously, the school had been entirely resident. Now, the number of residents was to remain the same, while the number of day pupils was to increase rapidly. By 1960, the enrolment was to be two hundred and thirty with only sixty-four residents. What was the attraction of Chetham's to the new kind of parent, many of whom were willing to pay fees?

One factor was the size of the school. It was felt that more individual attention would result where numbers were small, particularly in comparison with the much larger direct-grant schools. For some parents, the link with the Cathedral which was being developed was attractive. For others the offer of a free place under schemes approved with the local authorities could be a determining factor. Manchester undertook to provide for ten free places, and Salford for three. Bolton, Lancashire and Derbyshire also helped from time to time. There were also a dozen scholarships and exhibitions available under the Chetham's and Nicholls' Trusts. Even being situated in the centre of Manchester could be an attraction because travel from home would not be too complicated. The increasing musical reputation of the school would attract some parents, but music was not a determinant of entry, merely one of the factors to be taken into consideration.

Probably eleven-plus selection was the most important factor influencing parental choice. There was always the possibility that a boy might not be successful in the examination and yet pass the entrance examination into Chetham's. The entrance examination was not of a low standard, but the selection process was not as rigid as the eleven-plus itself and the competition was not so intense. Even as far afield as Rochdale, which was outside the scholarship range for the school, Chetham's became one of the options for a family which was not wealthy and yet was prepared to pay fees and daily travelling costs for the eldest boy in 1953. 'I have a suspicion that my parents doubted whether I would have passed the eleven-plus. So I sat the entrance examination and passed. Later, I became well aware of the sacrifices my parents were making on my behalf. There were many boys in my year in a similar position. When we were revising for our O levels I remember how we worked out how much it had cost our parents to have us educated at Chetham's over the five years. It was on our minds a great deal, and no doubt served to spur on our revision. If we didn't get O levels, all that expenditure would be a dead loss.' It would be absurd to generalise from a particular example, because each decision would vary from family to family, but applications for entry into Chetham's need to be related to educational options open to parents in the 1950's.

Much would depend on how well-known the school was. 'I had heard of Chetham's of the old days when there were fights with the boys from Manchester Grammar School. But nobody in their right mind sends their child through a small door (even the Gateway!) because of their fascination with the past. My son had already been accepted for a place in a school near

Oxford with a fine academic record. We also considered Manchester Grammar School for which his primary headmaster thought there would be no difficulty in passing the entrance examination. Then I met an old boy of Chetham's. He had all the care, courtesy and charm which we later found to be the hallmark of so many old boys of Chetham's. We visited the school, attended concerts and saw the boys. I was glad there were no musical tests then, for my boy would never have stood a chance. We did not think that the tuition was likely to be as good as at the school near Oxford but we have never felt that we had made the wrong decision. Chetham's became a large part of our lives.'

A strong relationship between parent and school was a vital part of the reorganisation of the school. No longer did a mother appear on an 'election' day, complete with carpet-bag, to be told that she could visit on certain restricted days after her boy was in the Hospital. The boys who, in 1952, were already in the school and had been elected by petition, had to adjust to being with an increasing number of boys, mostly day boys, who came from different home backgrounds and who, because of the change in entrance requirements, were capable of greater academic concentration. As far as Harry Vickers was concerned, all boys were to be treated in the same manner, regardless of different backgrounds or mental ability. He knew of the sacrifice some parents were having to make, equivalent to the 'painful and industrious' parents who were the beneficiaries under the terms of Humphrey Chetham's will. 'It is hard to believe that Humphrey Chetham would look with anything but favour on the institution which is developing out of his foundation. With more than half his boys receiving some financial assistance the House Governor believes that his school continues as a 'democratic, classless, family-size society', to serve the wishes of its founder as they can best be served in the twentieth century.'[1]

In 1952 there were no facilities for providing a grammar school type of education – no separate classrooms, only the 1878 Waterhouse schoolroom divided by a glass partition. Builders moved in while entry numbers increased. The strict

1 W. L. Webb, *Daily Telegraph* (1955).

discipline and the enforced daily routine from the days when all the boys were resident were continued and came as something of a shock to day-boys straight from a local primary school. 'The first day is so vivid in my memory. I can smell the uniform, and I can smell the building. It was a beautiful crisp morning, just the first sharpness in the air. I arrived in this ancient yard and we were lined up for inspection in a curious military way, where people were bawled at and made to march in step and line up in straight lines. A prefect would inspect shoes, hands and tie, and this prefect always thought you would be dirty behind your ear. He 'had a fiendish trick of grabbing the bottom of your ear to look behind it, and this happened on the first day. We were put in the old schoolroom because the new block had not yet been built. In winter it was cold and I remember we all got a rocket once for sitting there with our scarves and gloves on. I've never worked in such cold conditions as that big, high schoolroom'. (1953).

The first sixth form emerged in 1955 when the grammar school block had been completed, one boy on the arts side and two boys studying the sciences. The teaching staff had increased from three in 1951 to ten, comprising three junior school teachers for the eighty three boys aged seven to eleven, and seven for the one hundred and seventeen boys in the main school (one each for mathematics, English, French, Latin, history, and the sciences and art/handicraft). There was no specialist music teacher on the staff.

It was not numbers but tradition that moulded the ethos of Chetham's, even in its grammar-school phase. Change there certainly was. but continuity was stronger. There would be variables dependent on whether you were a resident, a day-boy, a junior or a chorister, but once within the walls and through the archway, you became a Chetham's boy.

> Everything was so old, it was like an authentic stately home. You went over cobbles under the gatehouse as if you were going into a castle. There were two old ladies sitting in the needle-room with starched white aprons and mob-caps darning the linen. In the Baronial Hall you sat at medieval tables as if you were a serf. Everywhere else everyone had a Headmaster, but here it was a House Governor and everyone called him 'Boss'. I suppose it's this

contrast with going to a primary school at seven. By the time you are eleven you know everyone in the school and you are in the football team. You are somebody. Then you move from being a king of one castle to being an absolute nothing in another. Chet's was so different from everything I had expected. It was like *Tom Brown's Schooldays.*

Each morning, day boys would arrive to find that the school had already been in operation for some time. Residents had been roused at 6.30 a.m., had stripped their beds, gone downstairs to join the queue for toilets and washbasins, returned to their dormitories to make their beds, and had dressed. Everybody had to be out of the dormitories and wash-house by 7.00 a.m. Then followed either a music practice or a trade. Everyone knew which came first. The boiler no longer needed to be banked up because oil-heating had been introduced, but the fire in the ingle nook in the Baronial Hall needed attention in the winter months. The ashes would be cleared out, coke obtained from the stove across the yard, and then the fire would be lit and kept going. A new trade was cleaning prefects' shoes. There would be litter-picking with particular attention to the sand and gravel in the cobbled areas. Music practice took place wherever practicable, but this was difficult because of restricted accommodation. Dormitories were out of bounds. Boys who had to practise would be with their instruments for half an hour and then move into a trade, while others who had been doing a trade would move into practice for the next half hour.

Then came the 7.45 bell for the second wash of the morning. 'Our lives were run by bells.' The 7.55 bell was for the line-up for breakfast parade. Shoes had to be polished, stains on blazers removed, trousers properly adjusted, hands and neck to be clean, tie properly tied, and any other detail corrected. Clothing was still numbered, with the Head Boy as Number One, and then alphabetically through each year down to the lowest number. The number was kept throughout the year, and it also appeared on the towel rack in the wash-house. After inspection came the march in to the allocated tables in the Baronial Hall, with a sung grace before and after each meal. Breakfast was no longer two slices of bread and margarine and a drink, but there could be bacon, eggs, scrambled eggs, fried bread, bread and butter and marmalade. Boys were no longer engaged in buttering bread as one of the trades, and meals were prepared by the catering staff. One boy from each table would act as a server, and the resident staff would be served at high table. There was a rule of silence while the meal was in progress and care taken to see that nothing was left on the plates.

Little seemed to have changed within the school, but even so old a school as Chetham's could not withstand the educational change outside its walls. Attention was being given to the education of the fifteen to eighteen age group, the very group which had been added to Chetham's in 1952, and with the Crowther Report came the explosion which was to transform higher education in England.

> We could not as a nation enjoy the standard of living we have today on the education we gave our children a hundred or even fifty years ago. If we are to build a higher standard of living and – what is more important – if we are to have a higher standard of life, we shall need a firmer educational base than we have today. Materially and morally, we are compelled to go forward.[2]

New universities provided unprecedented opportunities, and grammar school sixth forms were expanding. In the classroom, sixth-formers were encouraged and expected to develop a critical attitude in their studies. Learning by rote was being replaced by learning through understanding, and, at least in theory, entrance to university was linked with individuality. Would the conformist training which had previously worked so effectively for the under fourteen year-olds be appropriate for the fifteen to eighteen age group? It is perhaps not surprising that at Chetham's, while there continued to be an outward conformity, there also developed an inner rebellion reflecting the general change in the pattern of society. 'All teenagers clash with adults, and in the youth culture of the Beatles era it was fashionable to rebel. This led to a feeling of tension, but that tension gave urgency to all that was going

2 Report of the Central Advisory Council for Education – England. *15–18*. (H.M.S.O. 1959), p. 3.

on. It did not take away from the sense of adventure and purpose.'

There was so much to do, so much to achieve, and so much to share! Mondays were debates. 'They gave you a sense of adulthood in that you were developing something not in the tight structure of a lesson. You were also doing something with your name on it, and it made you feel it was a more adult contribution to the school than otherwise.' Tuesdays and Thursdays would be rugger practices. Wednesdays would be the Science Society. It didn't matter if you were on the Arts side, there was always something of interest, and in any case, little would happen if everyone didn't join in because numbers were so few. Fridays were special if you were lucky enough to be one of the twenty who had earned the right to be a member of the Renaissance Society. Formed 'to further a keen interest in literature by means of discussion, reading and creative writing', it published its own poetry magazine which received favourable reviews from John Betjeman, Edmund Blunden, Lord David Cecil, T. S. Eliot, Robert Graves, John Lehmann, C. Day Lewis and Norman Nicholson. Here in 1960 was a school which after only eight years was receiving wide acclaim.

In so small a school (two hundred and thirty boys in 1960 aged from seven to eighteen), orchestras, societies, sports fixtures, swimming achievements and concerts could not happen unless everyone took part, whether skilled or not, or even whether they wanted to or not. In 1963 the Three Peaks (Ben Nevis, Scafell and Snowdon) were climbed within a twenty four hour limit, with parents providing transport. Three years later, after training in a local lake, a team of six swimmers crossed the Channel in difficult weather conditions. Opportunities were provided and were avidly seized.

Academically, achievement was more average than exceptional because the emphasis was on all-round development rather than specialism, yet examination results were quite high for a one-form-entry grammar school. In 1966, the twenty nine candidates at O level had an average pass rate of over five O levels. Of the seventeen school-leavers after A levels, six went to study Arts, five to study science (including two who studied Medicine) at universities, and six went to colleges, two

·of which had a music specialism. For both pupils and parents, the school had purpose and vitality.

It became personified in Harry Vickers himself, seemingly tireless and always willing to venture into new territory. Stories of his eccentricities and humour abound, as they do of other Heads of schools where important change was taking place. 'Boss', as he was nicknamed was always resident, always available and always alert to any shortcomings. His views were well known because every opportunity was taken to express them, particularly after the evening meal and in long sessions with senior pupils. The correction of younger pupils by their seniors became institutionalized. Prefects would 'slipper' boys whose behaviour was regarded as unacceptable. Such practices may have continued to the mistaken image of Chetham's as a sort of public school and not a conventional day and boarding grammar school. There was no fagging and the House system operated in name only on a Sports Day. Courtesy to older people and to ladies, the opening of doors for other people, personal cleanliness and smartness were the order of the day, and senior boys were expected to set the example and enforce it. 'I couldn't comprehend the scale of Chet's. It was far more public school than I ever expected. The rules were far more stringent than in other schools. It was a cross between a church and a prison. Eventually, after being apprehensive, I became proud of the place. There was tremendous spirit. You just got used to the ropes and steered clear of trouble. The place engendered a superiority which manifested itself in a number of ways. I came to love that idiosyncratic institution with all its faults and regimentation.'

The school became even more attractive after the issuing of Circular 10/65 by the Minister of Education requesting local authorities to submit plans for the elimation of selection into separate and different types of school at eleven-plus. 'My parents sent me to Chetham's principally to avoid the local comprehensive school in Glossop. I would have been in the first year's intake. Father kept an open mind about the comprehensive. He had no political axe to grind but wondered how standards could be maintained if numbers were trebled. He went to all the preliminary meetings. The headmaster designate extolled the new school building, reserving his highest praise for the design of the enormous chimney that had been built larger than necessary to 'blend in' with mill chimneys in the valley that it overlooked. Father had a deep affection for his mother who had been a mill-girl from the age of four-teen, working ten hours a day and walking a six miles round trip to do it. She was not a profane lady but she once com-plained to my father about 'them bloody chimneys'. The head-master designate had wandered into an emotionally charged area, so I took the Chetham's entrance examination.'

Chetham's, then, could be regarded as an alternative to a comprehensive school, and it may have been logical to think so, bearing in mind that in the mid-1960s parents would be uncertain as to the effect of the comprehensive system on their children. From a sociological point of view, it would seem that Chetham's, in consequence of the divisiveness in educational provision under the 1944 Education Act, had become part of the middle-class establishment. It was still independent, and fees were charged! The reality was very different. The 1952 reorganisation of Chetham's stipulated a close relationship with the local education authorities, whose representatives were members of the School Committee and took an active part in decision-making. What was perhaps more significant was that over half the boys in the senior school were assisted in some way by the local education authorities. Far from being a separate and privileged middle-class establishment, Chetham's was very much dependent on local support and esteem. 'I had won a place at other direct-grant schools, but not a free place, and I was offered a free place at Chetham's by the Manchester authority. My father could not have afforded to pay fees, and if I had not been given a free place I would have gone to a comprehensive school. There had been extra tuition in the primary school before the examinations, and I already felt a dichotomy was beginning. It wasn't a social separation based on wealth. There are no big houses where I live. I was being plucked out of the normal mainstream com-prehensive conveyor belt and coming to Chetham's was like being put into the past. You went over cobbles into what seemed a castle, right in the middle of Manchester. I couldn't relate to the rules because I wasn't a resident. I had one foot outside because I was a day-boy, and felt neither one thing nor the other.'

Preparation for the eleven-plus selection examination was provided for in primary schools, and Chetham's was included among the grammar schools for which parents could express an option. Boys from families which could not afford the fees had their fees paid in part, or wholly, by the local authorities according to an agreed scheme. This aspect of recruitment to the school fitted in with the intentions of the Founder as modified to fit in with educational change in the post-war world. The other link with the past was the former Chetham's boy who was House Governor, and who had done so much to bring credit to the school. It had become a tradition for Chetham's to be the only school which held its Speech Day in the Town Hall, and the sight of the Blue Coat uniforms on the Free Trade Hall platform at annual Camp Fund Concerts reinforced the impression that Chetham's and Manchester were inseparably united.

Financial support for the school from local authorities depended on the eleven-plus system, and without that support the Endowment would be facing serious difficulties in providing for the educational needs of the school. The ending of eleven-plus selection in Manchester raised a vital question: should Chetham's break with local authorities, go independent, and become a totally fee-paying grammar school? Having reconstructed a grammar school from the old Blue Coat school, no inconsiderable task in itself, Harry Vickers and the Governors had now to consider yet again another fundamental change. It is perhaps not surprising that, with the intentions of the Founder in mind, a scheme should emerge which would continue and broaden the links with local authorities so that children could continue, in the changed circumstances, to benefit from being at Chetham's. What perhaps could be surprising was that the initiative to change Chetham's into a co-educational school for musically gifted children should have come from a man who was himself a non-musician. It was the determination of Harry Vickers to ensure that Chetham's should still provide for children in need.

Cricket before 1900.
The library to the left, the original college building behind

Football in the 1930s

Chetham's brass band, 1896

The choir, 1956.
At this time Cathedral choristers became pupils at Chetham's

Humphrey Chetham presiding over the ruins of an air raid in December 1940

Founder's Day procession from the School to the Cathedral, about 1949

CHAPTER 5

Music before 1969

No provision was made for music tuition in Humphrey Chetham's will. Apart from hymn singing at meal times and at services, musical activity does not seem to appear until 1846 when a gift of 'twelve fifes and four drums with a view to forming a band for the amusement of the Boys' was accepted. A band was organised, supervised by a visiting bandmaster, and became a regular feature of the school. The warning was given 'that if annoyance is found to result from such band, the same to be discontinued at any time'.

By 1864, the House Governor was 'empowered to take the boys with their band to head the annual procession of Sunday school scholars in Manchester on Whit Monday'. New brass instruments were needed, but financial approval was not always forthcoming. In 1874 there was an authorised purchase of:

5 Cornets	£15 0s 0d
1 E-flat Bass	£6 6s 0d
3 Tenor Horns	£9 18s 0d
1 Baritone	£3 15s 0d
1 Euphonium	£4 10s 0d
	£39 9s 0d

but three years later the band was not 'allowed to accept engagements out of school hours with a view of making the Band self-supporting and more efficient'. When the revenues supporting the Hospital were in decline, it was considered 'undesirable to expend so large a sum in the purchase of musical instruments but there is no objection to the House Governor arranging a concert in order to raise the necessary funds' (1891). Another request for additional instruments was refused in 1906, but the House Governor was authorized 'to accept engagements for the Boys' Band at fees which would be applied in repaying the cost of the new instruments'.

The Chetham's brass band would be hired out for special

occasions, for weddings and for royal visits. 'When the Prince of Wales visited Manchester, we were in the procession and as we marched past the saluting base near the statue of Queen Victoria in front of the old Infirmary, I nearly blew my inside out, due to my patriotic zeal and great love of music. Once a year we had a great treat. Embarking on a steamer at the Victoria Landing Stage which was across the road from the Cathedral, we sailed down the river Irwell as far as Trafford Docks, where we disembarked and marched to the Botanical Gardens, which were then one of Manchester's attractions. Our band played both during the voyage and in the Gardens but the thing we most looked forward to was the picnic tea with which we were always provided before returning to school via the Irwell' (1905).

The band, which had more or less to be self-supporting, was an activity in a resident school which took the boys out of the place and gave an outlet for their creativity. The musical skills were developed at evening practices, and warm relationships developed between bandmasters and the school. One, who was a former pupil, 'expressed the wish', when he died in 1902, 'that his trombone (with case) should be sent to his old school for the use of the Chetham Boys'. When funds were needed either for maintaining the number of boys in the Hospital or for making it possible for them to have a seaside holiday, the band would be available. Camp Fund concerts became a regular feature when parents and friends would come to the old schoolroom, visiting artists would entertain, the band would play and the boys would sing hymns and popular choruses. In this way, Chetham's was acquiring a local reputation as a school where music was part of its general life, although the only music being taught in the school was of the standard being produced at elementary schools.

The band was discontinued in 1926, and a quarter of a century was to pass before instrumental music began again. The reason for this was that after a reorganisation which allowed boys from Chetham's to attend outside grammar and central schools, there would not be enough time for band practice, which had to give way for more academic work: 'that in view of the changes in the reorganisation of the School, and the need for the time given to the training of the thirty-five boys in the Band for work of greater educational value, the Band should be disbanded'.

The daily singing of hymns at meal-times, and at concerts, gave a special quality to singing. There were no choristers at Chetham's until the reorganisation of the school in 1952. 'I must mention Christmas-time because although parents weren't invited, we used to have an evening meal, turkey and all the trimmings. We would be singing carols, and we would all be with our uniforms on, not long coats but the short ones. One carol I remember was *The Christmas Tree*: 'The Christmas tree is sparkling with light, and tapers twinkle on faces bright'. Another was the *Wassail Song*, but we had our own words:

> God bless the Governor of this house!
> Likewise the Matron too!
> And all the little Chetham's boys
> Around the table too!
> Love and joy come to you!

I never understood the *Boar's Head* carol because the verse was in Latin, but we sang it. It was all learned by tonic sol-fa, we didn't sight-read music. I only wish we had done sometimes. It was all in three parts, you can imagine about ninety-odd boys singing three parts. The Hall used to be decorated up, we had a Christmas tree with Christmas lights on. It was a really happy time. Governor always seemed to be in a good mood at this time. The morning after we all went home for Christmas leave (1938).'

Although there was no instrumental music and the singing was limited in range, when the boys returned from evacuation in 1948 the school acquired a high reputation for its music within a decade. How did this come about, bearing in mind that the new House Governor was a non-musician, and that no teaching staff were appointed for musical duties in this period?

Four interacting factors brought about the change. The framework was provided by the decisions made by the feoffees in fulfilling the intentions of the Founder in the changed educational circumstances of the post-war world. The close relationship which developed with the Cathedral enabled choristers to be educated at Chetham's, thereby providing a musical nucleus within the school. The incredible versatility and drive of the Handicrafts teacher made possible the growth of musical enterprise inside the school. Lastly, the determination of the new House Governor to bring the school into the twentieth century enabled boys to strive the achieve their full potential, particularly where music was concerned.

Since the seventeenth century, feoffees had preserved the school, administered the trust and ensured continuity. It could well have been the end of the road in 1945 but the decision was made, in spite of many difficulties, to proceed with reorganisation. A new management committee was formed which included representatives of local education authorities, the Ministry of Education and the Cathedral,[1] and the 1952 document approving the change made special mention of choristers: 'arrangements may be made for boys to be members of church choirs and to sing therein'. In this way, a junior school came into being in addition to the grammar school, thereby giving a musical foundation to the grammar school.

In any group of people collectively engaged in decision-making, while a consensus determines what is to be done, there is often an inner group on whom the responsibility for making proposals falls, so that their initiative gives a sense of direction to the decisions being made. At this time, there were three feoffees who could be regarded as guiding the school into its musical future while at the same time making sure that all was being done to improve all aspects of school life. Without in any way belittling the work of the committee as a whole, it would seem appropriate to mention who they were. Dennis N. Midwood had been a feoffee since 1927 and had made it his business to know practically every boy in the school. C. G. Boddington became a feoffee in 1935 and had similar concern for the welfare of each boy. The Midwood and Boddington families were well known for their devotion to public service.

1 The School Committee consisted of (a) thirteen nominated members, eight by the feoffees, three by the Trustees of the Nicholls' Hospital Trust, one by the Dean and Chapter of Manchester, one by the Ministry of Education and (b) four representative members, two by the Manchester City Council and two by the Association of Education Committees).

The third was Francis Willink, a member of the Hallé Concerts Society Committee, who had considerable experience in educational and welfare work. They gave freely of their time, energy and goodwill, and their influence was considerable in the city, for Chetham's was still very much a Manchester heritage.

Being a feoffee could sometimes be a family matter. 'I suppose it was in my blood in that my father was made a feoffee in the Thirties, and one can't live in a family without getting involved with what's going on around. I knew what was going on from what I heard my father talking about at home. The appointment of Harry Vickers as House Governor brought terrific enthusiasm and drive into the place which stimulated anybody who was there and who had the interest in trying to make Chetham's what it is today. There were terrific problems and he needed support. There was no money, the buildings were out of date, the conditions were appalling. When I was invited to serve on the committee I was thrilled because I'd had Chetham's in my blood since I was a child, and loved music. I was an ex-organ-scholar at Trinity, Cambridge and the thought that music might become part of the scheme at Chetham's excited me as a young man coming from university and being thrust into the business life of Manchester. Gerry Littlewood, the Handicraft man, collared me in for three days a week at lunch time to go and train the junior choir, and I did that for five years.'

'Gerry Littlewood, the handicraft man' had arrived at the school in the summer of 1949, straight from the armed services and training college. Appointed to teach art and crafts, he found a workshop stacked with damaged timbers which he had to clear so that there would be room to teach. The timbers were carefully examined and, where suitable, not destroyed. 'I have now at home,' a former pupil says, 'a pipe rack and a table lamp. I shall never part with them; they were made after the war, and after I'd left school, in the workshop, from pieces of war-damaged oak, which for about three hundred years were part of an oak chest.' Violins, also, were to be made later from salvaged and seasoned timber.

While in the Army Educational Corps, Littlewood had heard preposterous stories about a 'Dotheboys Hall' type of school in Manchester, told by a colleague who had been at Chetham's since the age of eight. When he became a resident master there, he learned the truth of the legends. 'It was an era of parades – wash-parade, bath-parade, laundry-parade, shoe-parade, and haircuts.' It was soon to become a music-parade.

He had not been trained at a music college, and possibly this lack of experience in school music was a benefit because no one who had such experience would have plunged so recklessly into starting an orchestra in conditions as they were in 1949. That blindness proved to be a positive asset. It was a professional rather than an educational approach. He brought with him six violins, two cellos and a clarinet, his personal property, and distributed them among the senior boys. The availability of the instruments and his ability as a tradesman to repair them removed any initial doubts. 'Those instruments passed through several hands before they found permanent owners. The older boys did not settle down to the hard practice and discipline required to master a stringed instrument. For them, after about a fortnight, the instruments were only fit for girls to learn. Football was more in their line. Smaller boys were now able to get a look in.'

The first appearance of the tiny orchestra was at the Christmas puppet show, 1949. Norman Cocker, the organist at Manchester Cathedral, was present and took interest in the emergence so near to the Cathedral of a school where musical training was being developed. More than two years were to elapse before official sanction was to be given to Chetham's as a grammar school when 'arrangements may be made for boys to be members of church choirs and to sing therein'. Meanwhile, foundations were being laid.

The school was in no financial position to purchase instruments on a large scale. Advertisements were placed in the *Manchester Guardian*, the *Manchester Evening Chronicle* and the *Manchester Evening News*, and some instruments arrived in response to these appeals. Some of the new boys brought their own instruments with them. One mother bought a simple system clarinet: not very expensive, not very good, not very useful, but at least it was a start for her son.

In 1949 there were but two members of staff in addition to

Littlewood, because the school was still small. Both were resident, as also was Gerald Littlewood, and to all three it was natural to give all they could to help the school which, in a way, was their family. The purchase of an instrument for one of the boys, a replacement for a broken violin bow, the duplication of orchestral parts through photostat equipment – these needs were attended to without any charge to the limited school funds, as also was the training and development of swimming and rugby at the school. Harry Vickers, the House Governor, was a non-musician, but he responded readily to the enthusiasm for music engendered by the growth of musical activity. 'A school in the heart of a city has problems of its own. We are happy that no boy has ever been involved in a road accident coming or going to school, but the playing-fields we use are a bus ride away, so we must substitute some other activity to occupy the boys in the evenings. Music is our main solution.' This may well have been an initial reason, but the development of music potential in the children under his care became an essential part of his work.

The orchestra became the method for training the individual. Rather than: 'I have learned the violin a bit, so I'll join the orchestra', it was: 'I have joined the orchestra in order to learn how to play a violin'. Every score would be individually tailored to the ability of each boy. Norman Cocker wrote parts prodigiously for hours on end so that an orchestral rehearsal was like a planned lesson; but instead of planning a lesson for a class, it was planned for twenty-four individuals who were all at different stages. The type of music was the kind of light music performed by professionals which allowed for the internal arrangement of parts to suit the capability of each performer without doing damage to accepted classical works. Cocker composed 'Chetham's Blues', 'Chetham's Rag', 'Chetham's Quickstep', and 'Chetham's Foxtrot' for the orchestra to play, and even used these pieces in the Cathedral at the Sunday morning services as in-going voluntaries and postludes after the service to get the musical idiom into the mind of the school as a whole. He was to be helpful to Chetham's for four years, and when he died in November 1953 his room was littered with the scores on which he had been working for the orchestra. He had even taken, at the age of sixty one, a Grade II Associated Board examination in violin playing to understand what it was like to be child learning how to play a violin.

Boys with no musical experience, and even with a hostility to music, were given opportunities to involve themselves with music. 'I was very much an uncultured youth, and wouldn't even deign to listen to classical music. I had to be forced to go to represent the school at the Cathedral when they had free tickets for a performance of the *Messiah*. I was not a musician and had no intention of becoming a musician, but when asked to be a double-bass player because the recently formed orchestra of nine lads needed one, I thought I'd have a go. So I became the school bass-player. It was a three string chamber bass, and after about twelve months, Gerald Littlewood added a string. He took it down to the workshop, made a brass ferrule and altered the neck.'

By 1953 music at Chetham's had come to be a part of the way of life, just like rugby, swimming and academic work. 'I was one of the poor boys from Salford whose authority paid my fees. It was normal to play an instrument. I was given a violin at the age of nine. I had no experience of music. Although music was stressed as an extra-curricular activity, there was no real pressure to make anybody join a choir or be in the orchestra. There were no ear tests. It just happened, and all the seven years I was there I was involved in music. I started in the junior choir and junior orchestra, and went into the senior choir, Glee Club and senior orchestra. It gave great pleasure and a deep sense of pride that I had been at Chetham's and played in the Free Trade Hall to a full audience.'

Ingenuity and improvisation were very much evident. There happened to be a cinema organ being dismantled locally and the friendly gesture was made whereby those parts of the organ providing tonal percussion were offered free to the school. In this way the orchestra was strengthened with a xylophone, glockenspiel, bells and marimba as well as non-tonal percussion such as cymbals, a triangle and bass and side drums. They were taken to the workshop to be fitted into appropriate stands so that they could be used for orchestral purposes.

As for music teaching, in these early stages no one received payment. In the evenings a student, later to be appointed to teach the sciences at the school, would accompany the 'singing' (the word 'choir' would not be accurate at this stage) and would compose pieces for the puppet play. From the Cathedral, Norman Cocker and the assistant organist, Douglas Steele, would freely give of their time and expertise in training the orchestra. At lunchtimes there would be drum lessons given by the grandfather of two boys in the school. He was working in a nearby office and was a drummer in the brass band movement. He brought a friend with him who was a clarinettist and gave free clarinet lessons. Another helper was an enthusiastic woodwind player who was constantly available, so that practically every evening and at weekends there was some musical activity somewhere, and all on a voluntary basis. Eric Davis, the subprincipal of the first violin section of the Hallé Orchestra and father of Michael Davis, a pupil who later became leader of the London Symphony Orchestra, was of considerable help in developing orchestra technique.

What had begun in a small way was now gathering its own momentum. In the absence of any music teachers, a monitorial system developed. Choristers developed more rapidly in this musical setting than others, and they were expected to teach others. Some of the senior pupils took over choir training and piano accompaniment. It would not have been possible for Gerald Littlewood, now plunged into the deep end, to cope with the many demands on his time without such help. When one of the boys was given the opportunity to have lessons with a professional musician, it was assumed and accepted that in return for this expense he would pass on the benefit accrued to other members of the orchestra.

Musical development at Chetham's was becoming noticed because in those days there were six daily newspapers circulating in Manchester, and the geographical position of the school gave easy access to the media. Local newspapers in the suburbs also gave coverage whenever groups from the school gave concerts. BBC radio and television broadcasts also contributed, particularly one Christmas programme which received national acclaim. Regular appearances at the Alderley Edge

Musical Festival and occasional choral links with the Hallé Orchestra drew attention to the school.

The Free Trade Hall annual concerts began in 1954 with a charity appeal for money to finance school building and help the Library. It speaks much for the daring of the School Governors to have booked a hall seating 2,500 when the only previous experience of fund-raising by concerts had been in halls seating not more than two hundred. There was so much goodwill in the city towards the school that not only was there a capacity audience, but the target of £75,000 was reached within two years. The concert took place in October 1954, with Sir John Barbirolli conducting Haydn's *Toy Symphony*. Part of the spectacle was the backcloth of the boys as they sat in their Blue Coat uniforms on the platform. The programmes that were devised for these concerts, which always included light music, always attracted large audiences, and it is known that the father of one of the boys, who was a charge-hand at a cotton factory, would sell about four hundred tickets as the weekly wages were paid out. Before Chetham's became a specialist music school, it was already filling the Free Trade Hall.

By 1953 twenty statutory choristers were at Chetham's, and another forty boys were in the Cathedral voluntary choir. Boys were not selected for any special musical ability, but the reputation for music-making attracted the attention of parents. Gerald Littlewood, who had a full-time teaching commitment in art and handicraft as well as being one of the two resident masters, now found himself, with voluntary help, coping with two orchestras and three choirs within the school as well as outside commitments for broadcasting and public concerts. In 1958 he became the first Director of Music at the school. The change of title meant little to him personally, but it signified the changed status of music within the school. Subjects taught in grammar schools have territories whose time frontiers are jealously guarded. An increase in time for music could only be at the expense of other subjects where preparation for external examinations could be seriously affected by a reduction in teaching time. It was revolutionary for music to be allowed so much time within the daily timetable as well as receiving stimulus in out-of-school hours. Diplomacy was needed to avoid clashes over poached territory, because music was to receive the same proportion as mathematics, English or languages. Without the backing of Harry Vickers and the cooperation of the rest of the teaching staff, music would not have developed in the way it did.

Each Tuesday and Thursday afternoon, as well as Saturday evening, were occasions for the senior orchestra to rehearse. The purpose was training in musical skills and not just preparation for a particular concert. The junior orchestra had mid-day hourly sessions also on Tuesday and Thursday, while the Glee Club met for rehearsal four days each week at 8.30 a.m. The Glee Club had about seventy voices, most having been trained in one of the Cathedral choirs and whose trebles formed the senior choir.

The first music room appeared in 1958. A place had to be found for orchestral practice because the yard was unsuitable in bad weather. Classrooms and laboratories had been provided in the new buildings, but no provision had been made for a rehearsal room. Another new building was beyond the means of the school, so the 1878 school room, designed by Alfred Waterhouse, was adapted. Its awesome height was divided horizontally to provide for the orchestra upstairs, while downstairs became an additional refectory. The school population had almost trebled and there was a need for the large number of day-pupils to have a place for the midday meal. The new music room was officially opened by Sir John Barbirolli. This development typified the way in which difficulties had to be overcome where resources were slender.

There was also the difficulty of how to afford specialist teachers to meet the needs of all the boys who wanted to learn. Or how to fit in all the private or group specialist lessons without interfering too much with academic tuition. Chetham's was not a music school, but a grammar school where music was but one of its many elements. Individual music tuition began to develop with a small group of visiting teachers, but no music fees were charged because music-making was a service provided by the school. There would be the rare occasion when a boy with exceptional musical ability might be selected on the basis of the eleven-plus examination and receive an educational grant.

Other boys would have other reasons for coming to Chetham's, although they too became involved in music-making.

My father left school when he was thirteen, and wanted me to have a good education. I was a nine-year-old and all the new boys sat down in a semi-circle. Gerald Littlewood went round asking us what we would like to play. Most replied violin or recorder because they seemed to know what was available. I hadn't been prepared beforehand, so when I was asked what I wanted to play, I said: 'A church organ'. There was absolute astonishment all round, and a complete silence. 'Can you play a piano?' I said, 'No'. 'Have you ever played a piano?' 'No'. 'Recorder for you, then' came the decision. I still remember the embarrassment. When I told him what I wanted to play I was made to look a fool and told to play a recorder. In fact, I went from recorder to clarinet. My first concert in the Free Trade Hall was playing 'Oranges and Lemons' in the junior orchestra. I still feel the majesty of being up there, performing before an absolutely packed house. Sweat was running down my fingers and getting into the recorder. That is where the collective image of Chetham's is, the one big family. We were all in it together.

Chetham's was little different from other grammar schools except that more was expected of its pupils because everyone had to be in it together. If you were a day-boy and in the Glee Club and orchestra, as most senior boys were, you would leave home to be in time for an 8.30 a.m. practice before school began. There would be orchestral practice twice a week during school hours. Out-of-school activities would mean that you would not be back home until about 8.00 p.m. Saturday mornings would be occupied with rugby or cricket matches, and Saturday evenings with orchestral practice or concerts. "School became the whole of social life which revolved more round the school than it did around home. I also came to attach more importance to the corporateness of music. For me it was always more important than in team games, which have always been held up as that sort of discipline. Orchestral playing demands more discipline and team effort to a higher degree of sophistication than team games."

We have seen how a Hospital School became a grammar
school. What we have been unable to see is all that went on
for the change to take place. Everyone involved seemed to be
filled with the constructive urge to create. Music was but a
part of the total picture. Whenever the point was raised as to
how far music training at Chetham's would contribute to a
career in music, the answer was that such a purpose was not
the intention for including music in the curriculum. Music was
a normal part of education, and proficiency obtained through
performance was the result of individual effort, rather than a
special gift. If someone went on to be a musician, all well and
good, but he would be no different from others who were to
follow other careers. What was shared was an intensive period
of growth. The history of the school made its unique contribution, the enthusiasm of the teaching staff played its part, but
the greatest influence came from the mulling over of the problems of children into the early hours, night after night, by two
dedicated, and some might think eccentric, individuals, Harry
Vickers and Gerald Littlewood. War-damaged oak was being
turned into pipe-racks and violins, a modern version of swords
into ploughshares.

CHAPTER 6

Why a music school?

One answer to the question, why a music school?, could be
that Chetham's was moving in that direction anyway. Change,
however, can never be as simple as that! There was a political
dimension in that the change was part of the general reconsid-
eration being given to secondary education after experience
of the operation of the 1944 Education Act. In 1952 the current
of educational reform had been flowing in a direction which
would allow for a Blue Coat school to become a grammar
school, but in the 1960s arguments for the ending of eleven-plus
selection and the replacement of grammar schools with comprehensive schools were moving the current in an opposite
direction. Circular 10/65 from the Department of Education
and Science had invited local authorities to submit proposals.
To contemplate the establishment of a a specialist selective
school at a time when egalitarianism characterised the
approach to secondary education would meet with criticism
and require a special justification. It would mean embarking
on an unknown course which would not be likely to receive a
general support, and in the difficult years of transition such a
frail craft might well founder.

No decision could be made without the approval of the feoffees, entrusted by Humphrey Chetham's will with responsibl il-
ity for the college site and buildings, and the maintenance of
the School and the Library on separate investment accounts.
The resources of the endowment had already been stretched
to the limit as a result of the changes that had already taken
place. We have seen how, so far as the school is concerned,
financial assistance from outside had been necessary when
resources were insufficient to meet the decline in rent values,
the burdens of inflation and the cost of altered educational
commitments. After 1908 there had been the public appeal for
funds, after 1926 educational cost had been lightened when
many Chetham's boys became outside scholars educated in

maintained schools, and after 1952 more than half the boys were to be receiving assistance from local educational authorities. By the mid-1960s, however, it became apparent that while local authority interest and support for musical development at Chetham's was developing, the reorganistion of secondary education on comprehensive lines would make it doubtful whether local authorities would continue to select children for support at Chetham's. The close link with the city of Manchester remained, but the ending of eleven-plus selection would mean the ending of an important part of the process by which the school had been sustained. If, however, the musical content of the school curriculum, which was already well known and admired locally, were to be developed further, and if the Manchester authority and others were to continue their support because of musical development within the school, then the financial strain could possibly be eased. Much would depend on consultation with local education authorities, particularly Manchester, and with the Department of Education and Science.

There was an alternative. Chetham's could 'go it alone' without local authority involvement, and become an independent school for fee-paying pupils, with some scholarships and exhibitions. Other schools with a charity foundations were moving in that direction and for Chetham's such a development had its attraction because of the excellent local reputation of the school. The opposite decision, however, was made and Chetham's was to move in a direction which would depend even more on local authority support. Even with continued local authority backing, the requirements for establishing a junior school of music would make financial demands well beyond the resources of the endowment. The decision could not have been made without a belief in the importance of music in education, a belief which was receiving considerable attention in the recommendations of the first Gulbenkian Report, *Making Musicians*, 1965.

This report had drawn attention to the inadequacy of musical education in Britain. Much of the report related to music colleges and higher education, but stress was placed on the need for the recognition and encouragement to be given to young children who had exceptional ability in music. It argued that in an ordinary school 'the timetable is too congested, and the really talented musician is too rare a bird for suitable arrangements to be made in it'. There should be 'systematic training in instrumental technique, and disciplined practice under expert tuition for talented children from the age of eleven for keyboard players and seven or eight for string players'. Three schools only were referred to as pioneering the education of musically gifted children: the Central Tutorial School for Young Musicians (twenty-one pupils), the Yehudi Menuhin School (thirty-one pupils), and the National Junior Music School (for a few pupils who were in the National Youth Orchestra but whose schooling could not satisfactorily be arranged elsewhere). Chetham's was not mentioned in the Report, although it was, in fact, already providing for the type of education recommended, and not only for keyboard and string players but also for wind and brass. It was Harry Vickers who suggested to the feoffees in 1967 that the school's role might be changed because of its reputation for the cultivation of musical attainment.

Chetham's was still a school whose purpose was rooted in the intentions of a Founder who wanted to provide for children in need so that they could be prepared for work. In 1952 these intentions had been adjusted to suit the changed educational and social pattern of a post-war world with the school becoming a grammar school, preparing for entry into the professions and higher education. Gerald Littlewood had demonstrated what could be done within the framework of a grammar school to foster the potential of musically gifted children. Attention had been drawn by the Gulbenkian Report to a new need, the need of a musical child. A step further in the direction of increasing musical content without appreciably disturbing the existing organisation and administration would conform with the intentions of the Gulbenkian Report. Talks began on these lines in 1967, but it was not until 1969 that the details were agreed and it became possible for Chetham's to begin to be a school of music.

In the interim, rumour flourished, questions were raised for which there could be no clear answer, and there was disquiet among those who feared that the change would be too severe a break with the past. There was widespread concern over all the changes in secondary education that were being generally contemplated, and Chetham's was no exception. The main fear was that academic standards would fall if additional attention were given to music. There was a Press leak in April 1968 which obliged Harry Vickers to meet with parents on four separate evenings to reassure them about the future of their children at the school. The difficulty was that no public announcement could be made until all the details had been agreed and sanction had been given by the Secretary of State. The questioning was endless and the answers, as is so frequent where the education of young chldren at a time of change is involved, were based more on hope than certainty. Would selection be limited to the very gifted? If so, would there be a sufficient number to justify the school? With no academic test for entry, how could academic standards be maintained? Would local authority support be forthcoming? What job prospects would there be for musicians? How much would a specialist music education cost? Should public money be spent in this way, favouring the few?

Chetham's was not alone in receiving attention because of its musical achievement. The training of musicians at all levels, particularly in music colleges, had featured in the Gulbenkian report. The plans for the merging together of the Royal Manchester College of Music and the Northern School of Music were nearing fruition. In Croydon, the possibility of providing boarding accommodation for members of the National Youth Orchestra, together with general education in schools maintained by the local authority, was being explored. The further development of a music specialism at Wells Cathedral School was receiving consideration. In all these discussions there was a common basis that musical children, in addition to their special needs, would also receive an education sufficient to stand them in good stead for employment in professions other than music. There was to be no 'conservatoire' type of training in musical virtuosity alone.

By September 1968 the point had been reached where a declaration of intent, as far as Chetham's was concerned, could be made. Parents were informed that in future 'all boys coming into both the junior and senior schools will be required to learn an instrument'. Parents were asked 'to ensure the regular and thorough practice by their children, and their attendance at practice and lessons, even though they may be outside the normal times'. It was a small step, a hint of the shape of things to come. At this stage, nothing further could be done until the complicated procedure had been completed. In his inimitable way, Harry gave the teaching staff his appraisal of the situation: 'Clearly, next year will be a time of frustrating inactivity, punctuated by periods of frenzied involvement. All this is very nebulous: we can only try to anticipate the early future at any one time. No one has any idea of the size of the potential demand, not to mention the possible effective demand. The transition period may well be as long as fifteen years, remembering that we are committed to provide for every single youngster who will be in the school in September 1969.' It was an accurate forecast!

In the spring of 1969 Palatine Buildings, which had been constructed as a railway hotel in |1843 and since adapted as an office block with a ground floor of shops, were purchased to provide temporary accommodation for girl boarders and practice rooms. The Calouste Gulbenkian Foundation gave £25,000 towards the cost, with another £5,000 coming from the Northern Arts and Science Foundation. The way was being prepared for the major change in September.

When September came, the pattern of unity among the pupils was replaced by a diversity which was made more apparent because the newcomers came in at different levels, not in one age group. Thirty of the fifty new pupils were girls ranging from the age of eight to sixteen. There were two hundred and fifty boys already in the school who had been admitted under the previous scheme. There were among them a minority of non-musicians, but the majority were involved in general musicianship. Instead of uniformity, then, there were the few girls intruding into a traditional male school, there were musicians and non-musicians, and even among the musicians there was a sharp distinction between the general musician and the high-flyer. Presiding over these changes, and

D

beset with all manner of political and financial pressures, was Harry Vickers. He had retained the paternalistic supervision which had characterised the days when he had been a boy at Chetham's. 'When I first met him he was like a very stern Victorian uncle speaking to a little boy before going to bed. It was the day of the interview and he saw me without my parents. "Now your father's out of the way," he said, "let's get down to brass tacks. What do you really like doing most?" When he said this, I just felt that I was going to be happy there. There was sternness, but there was also a tender, caring attitude.' Another voice: 'Everyone called Mrs Vickers "Matron", but she was "Mum" to me. It was all very formal, with traditions which I thought were magical and wonderful – such things as bell-ringing, lining-up for lunch and being inspected, singing *To Be a Pilgrim* at every important assembly, even the slippering by prefects. I didn't look on Chetham's as a school where I was being educated. It was a home, even though I was a day-boy.'

But there were those in 1969 who felt that the community of which they were part was being undermined. 'As I grew older I identified with the school, yet here were what seemed to be joy-riders. Music was their meal ticket. They had not gone through the struggle, the pride, the passion which was, to our way of thinking, in the heart of Chetham's. They seemed to us a danger to the traditional values of the school.' There was a tradition of prowess on the rugby field. The thirteen-year-old boys felt threatened. 'The regime which I was only just beginning to understand was being diluted. I would never get the opportunities that I thought I had earned by weathering the storms in the early years to get into a position where the school would be the same as when I started. There was a feeling of slipping away, not just because girls came in, but also musicians and non-sportsmen, and people who were so different from the standard type of entry in the days before 1969. There had been musicians who played rugby, but now the word 'musician' took on a special derogatory meaning as a 'non-rugby-playing person'. It was a way of distinguishing 'our school', the tough, physical school we had grown used to, from the wave of these others who in time would submerge us.'

One of the newcomers, later to have a career as a professional violinist, understood the situation and took up rugby. 'But one or two of the other musicians didn't, and suffered a bit in consequence. In my opinion, the main concern of Harry Vickers was not their academic work, nor what they did in music, important though these were, so much as social development. He took great pains to fit me for society, and now that I am a professional musician making my own way in life I feel I benefitted from what he did. He gave me a sense of independence. You had to stand firmly on your own two feet because we were in the middle of a great deal of animosity.'

From an eleven-year-old girl's point of view, 'the main change was that the school was going coeducational, not that it was going musical. We girls had much trouble in being accepted. We hardly spoke to the boys in the first few weeks. Boys were not happy because we were called by our Christian names, while they were still called by their surnames. We kept ourselves very much to ourselves and used to stay in cloakrooms during break or lunchtime rather than venture out into the boys' world.'

We can only guess at what that boys' world entailed, and no doubt there would be variations according to age. 'I can't believe now how naïve I was when I was thirteen. I had had no contact with girls before. Of course, I had sisters, but all they had done was jump on my sandcastles. Suddenly, girls came. The whole school fell in love with the older ones. The younger ones were regarded as a bit of a nuisance. Girls made me desperately unhappy just by their very appearance. I didn't know what to do, or how to act, and I'm not surprised that none of them found me attractive. When 'flare' trousers were the rage I had to have a pair even though they were too wide, so I would put a physics book down my back and make sure I wore a blazer all the time to cover the book. We couldn't understand why they couldn't play rugby, or why they couldn't have a tussle on the yard. These strange creatures who had invaded us were beyond our understanding.'

One of these strange creatures was a sixteen-year-old girl who came in, as it were, from the outside, in September 1969. She appreciated what was customary at Chetham's, but at the same time was impatient for the future. 'Paradoxically, Chet's is both steeped in tradition and is very forward-looking. The former is found on occasions like Founder's Day when the boys in Tudor uniform are now joined by the girls in procession round the Cathedral, with the festive spirit enhanced by carrying posies of flowers. But less happily, the fact that Chet's is steeped in the past is reflected in the backward-looking attitudes of those who, despite the usual grumbles, remain complacently satisfied with the status quo.' This was plain speaking, and her assessment of the situation was remarkably clear-sighted: 'there is a need for a development plan which will increase the facilities and provide extra accommodation; there are difficulties in making the new system of coeducation workable, especially as so many are unwilling to give girls parity of status; the need to accommodate music-making without allowing scholarship to suffer; and above all the problem of ensuring, as far as possible, that individual pupils do not suffer in any way from being members of the school in this transitional period.' Her words accurately describe the situation as it was in 1969.

A junior school of music had been authorised by the Department of Education and Science. There were three stipulations: entry was to be solely by audition; the school would be coeducational; there would be no religious test. Although there had been no religious tests during the grammar school period, the habit had developed for Roman Catholics and Jews not to apply, and the school, with its close link with the Cathedral, had become identified with the Anglican church, although there were Nonconformist families with children there. The main changes were the ending of academic selection and the admission of girls.

Manchester and Salford had agreed to continue to support pupils, and the general approval of other local authorities was reached on the understanding that selection would be in consultation with music advisers. Fifty pupils were admitted after audition. Some pupils who were already in the school but had not been assisted by local authorities were also auditioned and were able to receive financial help on grounds of their musicality. In the early stages auditions sometimes became the subject of criticism, not because the Director of Music had low standards, but because the school was not yet sufficiently well known for all applications to be of a high standard. Also, until accommodation and appropriate tuition was of the requisite standard, children of exceptional ability were unlikely to apply. Chetham's was still only known locally, so the area of recruitment was a limited one. In consequence, admission to the school in a musical sense was of mixed quality. A distinction was made between general musicians, selected because in their primary schools they had revealed a keen interest in music, and the few who had shown exceptional ability. Manchester, for example, supported ten pupils so that the best ten selected themselves regardless as to whether or not they were deserving of a specialist musical education. Later, Manchester was to support only those who could demonstrably benefit from being at a specialist school. The general musicians were in no way to be held back because they had entered a specialist school. The cost of adapting to meet the needs of that specialism was to prove so high that it was many years before the specialism could be fully developed. While the change took place, full academic tuition continued, as had been recommended in the Gulbenkian report, and when this generation came to leave the school for non-musical careers they had benefitted from being in a community where music, which they valued, was being developed. In 1969 the purpose of the change was clear, but what was not so clear was how to devise the means to achieve that end.

CHAPTER 7

Years of difficulty

Let there be a fanfare for September, 1969!

> When the new term opened this week at Chetham's Hospital
> School, Manchester, the three-hundred-year-old boys' boarding
> school suddenly became the first of its kind in the country. With
> a headmaster who can't play a note and a self-taught director of
> music, the old charity school in the city centre has become Britain's
> only junior school of music open by audition to children from seven
> to eighteen. A £120,000 conversion has turned the interior of a
> Victorian warehouse attached into a stylish and comfortable hostel
> for girl boarders.[1]

Twelve years were to pass before there was certainty that a
junior music school had been established. In education, as in
other spheres, it is not possible to achieve change at a stroke.
The first five years were to prove particularly difficult, and
even after 1974 strenuous effort was needed to ensure, at a
time of accelerating educational costs and high inflation, that
the necessary development took place. Unlike the previous
change in 1952, it was not as if a local charity school was being
assisted to become a local grammar school with all the attractions that a grammar school then had. Support was now being
asked for something less easy to define. Opinion was divided
as to whether musical children should have a specialist education at all, even though recommended by the Gulbenkian
Report. There was also the strongly held opinion that a
specialist musical education should only be for string players.

Chetham's was setting out to provide an environment in
which musically gifted children, no matter what their instrument, would be able to develop their potential in a shared
musical experience (aural, choral, theoretical, creative and
academic) which would make them fuller musicians. The
Peacock Report (1970) to the Arts Council claimed that there
was a shortage of instrumentalists of a standard high enough
to meet the growing public need for quality performance

1 The *Sunday Times*

and had commended the work which was already being done at Chetham's. There were other ways in which music was being fostered, such as with local authority Music Centres, junior Exhibition schemes at colleges of music, and the attachment of a special Music Unit to the Pimlico School under the I.L.E.A. They were all part of satisfying a national need, but there was a hesitation about going as far as a specialist school. The appeal brochure drew attention to the fact that 'no other major establishment yet exists to meet the needs of these boys and girls, which needs have hitherto been neglected save in two valuable experiments in the south'.

Another doubt related to careers in music. The Gulbenkian Report itself had warned against too specialised a type of education, and had insisted on a general education as well, which would enable a child to have a career other than a musical one. The appeal brochure explained this aspect: 'The new Chetham's will not become a vocational training centre; some of its pupils will indeed become professionals – it is hoped of a high standard – some will become fine teachers, but some, too, will take into other walks of life enriched cultural interests and leisure skills which our modern society desperately needs'. If the specialist school were not going to produce musicians, what justification was there for the specialism, and why support it? Such a question may well have contributed to the early difficulties in gaining a wide support for the new venture. There may well also have been a reluctance to support the unknown, because the kind of specialism practised in other countries was alien to the general education pattern of Britain.

The feoffees had embarked on a risky venture. The endowment funds were in no position to provide for the heavy capital expenditure for additional music tuition and accommodation for boarding and practice rooms. There was a response to the appeal for funds, but nothing like on the scale that was needed. An approach was made to the Government but it was too early for support from that quarter. The possibility of a close relationship with the National Youth Orchestra was explored, but nothing materialised here. Everything depended on whether a sufficient number of properly qualified children would be supported and therefore be able to attend the school.

A publicity campaign had to be mounted to make the school more widely known.

Harry Vickers was relieved of some of his duties as House Governor, in particular the supervision of financial detail, so that he could travel and campaign for the school. Another decision in 1970 was to defer any further investment in the school until there was sufficient evidence that the junior music school was being nationally supported. This drastic remedy was forced unwillingly on the feoffees because it would have been irresponsible to have allowed the endowment funds to be run down on behalf of a school which had no future. It was to take four years before this financial restriction could be lifted. By 1971 there were eighty-five specialist pupils, and some thirty local education authorities were providing financial support. By 1972 there were one hundred-and-fifty music specialists out of a a school total of two-hundred-and-eighty and some fifty local authorities were financially assisting one hundred children. The remainder were fee-payers, and because of increasing school expenditure the fees had to be increased, although some help had come from the Leverhulme and Grocer's Charities. The showing on television of a fifty-five-minute documentary film *A Gift for Music* by Granada T.V. helped to gain a wider acknowledgement that the school existed.

Visiting music teachers for specialist pupils came in from the emerging Royal Northern College of Music in Manchester, from established orchestras and from London, while one or two pupils had to visit Leeds or Liverpool for lessons. Such pupils would, with travelling time, take the most part of a day for one lesson. The general pattern was for two lessons a week on a first instrument and one lesson on a second. There were some forty-five tutors engaged in musical education, with an academic staff of fifteen, and there was occasional friction between the two staffs, particularly over the encroachment of time. It was perhaps unfortunate that the academic teaching rooms and laboratories were located on one side of the school yard while music was confined to Palatine Buildings on the opposite side, making it less likely for meetings to take place to consider mutual needs and problems. Gerald Littlewood had the difficult task of preparing for a developed music tuition while not having the means to achieve it because of the restriction placed on expansion. A special Music Committee[2] was formed in an advisory capacity but nothing could be done until authorisation of the necessary expenditure was forthcoming.

A visiting professor[3] spent a month living inside the school in the autumn of 1972 and was able to see at first hand why there was a 'crisis of confidence at Chetham's'. He reported on the difficulties faced by the school. 'It is difficult to conceive an adequate musical education being given with greater parsimony. The school does not have a satisfactory concert room, having to make use of the existing gymnasium. The school does not possess its own organ. A fair proportion of practice rooms are uncomfortable and inadequate and they all require additional sound-proofing to come up to a standard appropriate for a junior conservatoire. Although there are pianos of varying quality, there is a need for a really expensive concert grand.' He quoted a saying of the House Governor at the time: 'My best service to the school is to keep a cheerful face.'

Both parents and teaching staff were concerned because the future of the school was uncertain. Some teachers left because it looked as if their particular subject would be regarded as less important as the school became more specialist. It did not seem as if academic staff of the calibre necessary for teaching at advanced level would be attracted to work in a school whose policy was a music specialism and whose pupils had no academic test on entry. For economy reasons, two teachers were made redundant. The disappearance of art and handicraft from the curriculum confirmed the worst fears of parents and some withdrawals were made from the junior forms. When the alternative CSE examination was introduced, Harry Vickers had difficulty in persuading parents that this step was not indicative of a decline in academic standards, but merely an adjustment, as in other non-selective schools, for the few pupils for whom the new type of examination was more suitable.

2 John Manduell (Chairman), Ida Carroll, OBE, Sir Keith Falkner, Professor Alun Hoddinott, Hector McCurrach, Joseph Weingarten, David Willcocks, CBE, Harry Vickers (ex officio), Terence Greaves (co-opted).
3 John B. Mays, Liverpool University.

In time, all these fears were not realised, academic standards were to rise and not fall, and academic staff of the appropriate kind were to come and stay, but the prospects were grim in 1972. Even so, the final verdict from the visiting professor was a favourable one. 'It is frequently said that Chetham's is a school with an especially strong family spirit. Some members of the school and some former members think this is often exaggerated, that it is a kind of myth born of wishful thinking and nostalgia for the past. As a visitor and guest I must say that I do not agree with this latter view. As is true of all schools and all institutions undergoing drastic change and reorganisation, there are inevitable flaws in the daily life at Chet's. But, when all that has been said, the school does emanate a distinctive ethos, composed of serious, balanced, amicable and cooperative attitudes on the part of the majority of staff and pupils. It is moreover as a school and not solely as a training ground for the musically gifted that Chetham's will be judged and will want to be judged. The autumn 1972 intake of new pupils, almost all of whom are musical, is said to be very satisfactory academically and a big improvement on the few previous years – an indicator coming at a critical moment, which seems firmly to indicate that the attempt to pioneer this combination of grammar and specialistic music is going to succeed.'

The corner was being turned, but real progress could not be made until the embargo on capital investment could be lifted, and in turn this could not happen until there was a sufficient number of supported children of the quality who would benefit from a specialist education. During these years some non-specialist children had been admitted, so there was a wide range within the school – non-musicians from the pre-1969 days, some general, as distinct from specialist, musicians, and even among the specialist musicians a few who could be regarded as exceptional.

Even for a high-flyer, for whom it might have been assumed that the school was most suitable, the stage had not yet been reached where the needs could be fully satisfied. 'I wondered whether it would have been better going to a normal school and fitting in my practice after the school day, as many people have done successfully. When I arrived I was placed in the top junior form because of my age. When I asked when my practice time would be, I was told that there was no practice time for juniors, so I was transferred to the senior school. Even there, practice time had not yet been knitted into the timetable and you would be withdrawn from an academic lesson for a music lesson. Yet there were considerable benefits, even though the school was still in an early stage of development. Percussion lessons, always important for a pianist, were something you wouldn't have in an ordinary school. Also, we had the experience of many concerts, which we would not have had elsewhere.' With only a minority of music specialists, the school was not yet able to make adequate timetable provisions. All tutors were part-time and the specialist children were taken out of academic lessons at the convenience of the tutor. Steps were being taken by Gerald Littlewood to rationalise the situation, and by 1974 instrumental lessons were being organised by the school on behalf of the pupils, and not by tutors at their own convenience. A system was being devised whereby all children, regardless of their music commitment, would have an uninterrupted and personal academic programme.

Side by side with a high-flyer would be a non-musician who was already in the junior school before 1969. Change had not yet affected him, and although he was to be withdrawn from the school by his parents in 1972 he recalls his four years at Chetham's as the happiest and most important years in his school life: 'You never wanted to go home. I'd spend five nights a week doing rugby and swimming training. Even though I was twelve, the school treated you as an adult. It was not so much what you learned in the classroom as what you learned out of it from mixing with all types of different people.'

In contrast with the high-flyer and the non-musician was the general musician, all three sharing a common social and academic experience but going their differing ways so far as music was concerned. 'I come from a very working-class background and my parents did not have anything to do with classical music. I got there by a fluke, by having a very interested primary school headmaster. I came to feel guilty that Manchester was paying thousands of pounds for me to have a specialist music training and I wasn't making the most of the opportunity. It was obvious at the outset that musically I was not of the calibre of some in the school. There was a girl in the second form whose Chopin was amazing, and when I compared myself with her and with others, I found I lacked the dedication to put in so many hours of concentrated practice to achieve so high a standard of performance. My interests were outside music because I am more academic. I may well have been the only one in my age group who did not take A level music, but the choice was left to me. It was not forced on us that we were going to be musicians. I took an active part in choral work which I loved, and still do, and like others in my category we have not lost our enthusiasm for music.'

The Music Committee had a series of meetings in 1973 and their report was issued in February 1974. Appreciation was expressed for the work which had been undertaken during the transitional period and recommendations were made to the feoffes regarding future staffing, accommodation and equipment. The decision to lift the ban on further capital expenditure was still being awaited and would depend on the quality and backing for the intake of pupils for the following September. It was at this juncture that two events occurred which were to mark the end of an era in the history of the school. The last House Governor was to retire and the Director of Music was to resign. Gerald Littlewood had already expressed the view that the appointment of someone who was better known might well be necessary for the sake of a national acceptance of the scheme. For Harry and Audrey Vickers, the strain of successfully undertaking a second major reorganisation of the school within the short space of twenty-five years was beginning to take its toll. He had done all he could to further a school to which he owed so much, and it was with this deep sense of loyalty that he decided to offer his retirement to make way for a younger man to complete the work to which he had devoted all his energies.

John Vallins became Headmaster in September 1974 having been Housemaster and Head of English at Cranleigh School, Surrey, for the previous ten years. He was not appointed as House Governor, and the change of title marked the end of an era in the history of the school. Originally, a Warden had been appointed to oversee the feeding, clothing and general welfare of the boys in the Hospital, but in time the title House Governor had come to be used for the person responsible for these duties. A House Governor did not teach, at least not on a regular basis. Until the time of Harry Vickers, a House Governor had been rather like an Overseer in general charge and removed from the day-to-day work in the school. All this changed with Harry Vickers who, while retaining overall responsibility for the welfare aspect of the school, so immersed himself in every aspect of the school that it became absurd to regard a House Governor as a remote being. He was very much a vigorous Headmaster, and in 1970 he had been relieved of some general responsibilities so that he could concentrate more on the school. It was natural for his successor to be a Headmaster and not a House Governor, particularly as some of the general responsibilities on the domestic side were now being undertaken by the Bursar.[4]

Perhaps 1974 rather than 1969 should be regarded as the year when Chetham's became a music school. It was the year when the last House Governor retired. It was the year in which the restrictions which had been imposed in 1970 were lifted. It was the year when two men who had so successfully prepared the way, were to leave the school to enable others to build on the foundations they had laid. Their achievement was considerable: a recognised music school had been established; some good professional musicians had resulted from the training at Chetham's; academic work had not been sacrificed; an effective tuition pattern was in operation; the goodwill of local authorities was being secured; and perhaps most important of all, although faced with the difficulties in dealing with children of mixed abilities, the most was being made of the potential of each child. The way was now clear to go ahead. Gerald Littlewood departed at first to undertake work in art and handicrafts and later to concentrate on what had always been his absorbing interest, and which had led him to foster music at

4 In 1977 the word 'Hospital' was removed from the name of the school. The new name 'Chetham's School of Music' would be more easily understood by outsiders and those associated with the school in the future, who would be unaware of the alternative meaning of the word 'Hospital'.

Chetham's in the first place, namely the making of violins. Unhappily, Harry Vickers suffered serious illness after retirment and was not able to witness the results of his work. From his retirement he had these memorable words to pass on: 'Exciting times lie ahead. What pleases me is the early likelihood of the increasing provision of services, equipment and accommodation, so long awaited, so hopefully planned by our team in days when the financial stringency of reorganisation meant that material progress had to remain a dream for the time being. In the end it will be the School itself which will forge its own future. About this, there need be no misgivings at all.' A moving tribute was paid to his memory when many former pupils and all associated with the school attended the service at Manchester Cathedral after his death on 12 November 1976.

The new Director of Music was Michael Brewer of Latymer School, London, but he did not take up his duties until January 1975. There was an interval which provided the new Headmaster with an opportunity to assess all the elements which had been evolving while the school was changing. The school was moving away from an established grammar education pattern to one which would allow a child to practise on an instrument for up to three hours a day, while at the same time having a balanced academic programme which, if the child so chose, would enable him to carry on to further education in a career other than music. It had to be a step-by-step approach as finance and accommodation made it possible for adjustments to be made. There was now sufficient recognition and support of the school to offer places only to those candidates who were able to satisfy the audition panel that they were of sufficient musical calibre to benefit from being in the school.

One reason for reluctance to support Chetham's had been the view that it was an élitist institution which was only paying lip-service to musical education. Some authorities were of opinion that the musical service which they were providing in their own locality was every bit as adequate as anything they felt that Chetham's could provide. Music advisers and other experts were invited to see for themselves what was taking place.

They often stayed for twenty-four hours, attending any lessons they wanted and talking freely with the children in the school It was a 'warts and all' experience which resulted in winning over advisors who previously had not been enthusiastic about the specialist education that was being developed. So much variety had previously been necessary that the progress towards specialism had not been sufficiently noticed. September 1975 witnessed the seventh intake of pupils by audition, so that for the first time the school could be regarded as almost wholly musical – almost, because there was still a small group of veteran pupils from the previous era who had survived the changes.

Their academic work had not been neglected but naturally they had felt more and more out of things as the school had changed. 'We were the people who never went to choir and never had music lesssons. I personally didn't feel isolated because these were friends whom I had known for ten years. It would be a strange feeling on a Friday morning. The five of us would be in the old College building and when we looked out of the windows the school was like a desert. Senior, intermediate and junior choirs, all the rest of the school, were elsewhere singing and we were the only five who weren't. Partly for fun and partly for protest, we formed a memorial choir of our own and named it in memory of one boy who had already left the school. He had always been the butt of everybody's jokes as a non-musician, although he took it in the best possible way. We wore special T-shirts on our own last day with his name printed on them followed by the words 'Memorial Choir'. To many the inscription would be meaningless, but for us it had a special significance.'

Others who were leaving had also lived through the changes and to some extent shared the feeling that the transitional period was drawing to a close. 'When I came to Chetham's it was not because I wanted to be a cellist. I went because I enjoyed music, was supported by a local authority and it was thought that I would benefit from being at the school. I did, and went on to university to study music. If children get into Chetham's today (1983) they will have already achieved a higher standard than we did in our day. They have much more of an idea of what they are letting themselves in for than when we went there.'

In 1978 over seven hundred enquiries were received about entry to the school. Two hundred and fifty of the candidates were auditioned and places were offered to fifty-eight, but difficulties were experienced in obtaining grants for all these pupils who were considered to need what a specialist school could provide. There had been a Parliamentary debate on the question of public support for specialist music schools in the light of a second Gulbenkian Report, but there was still no acknowledgment of the need to finance such schools nationally. John Vallins was convinced of the value of the specialism. 'We would never claim that every musically gifted child should be educated at a resident specialist school. Some of the most gifted will always thrive best at home or in non-specialist day-schools. Circumstances, personalities and the availability of outstanding teachers are all very variable factors. Music centres and the junior schools are clearly a vital part of the framework of opportunities available to young people. But, when all this is said, we also contend, and strongly, that resident schooling is the best for a significant number, and that the financial arrangements should not discriminate against this small branch of education which costs, nationally, little more than £1 million per annum.'

By 1978 sixty education authorities in England, Scotland and Wales were supporting two hundred and forty-six children at Chetham's, which was an encouraging advance, but there were seven children that year who could not come because their authorities refused discretionary grants and another three were offered grants which were not large enough to enable the successful candidates to take up their places. Scholarships and Educational Trusts helped, but in the end some children who had been adjudged as sufficiently exceptional to benefit from being at Chetham's were withdrawn. This anomaly was finally put right when, after a report on the school by the Department of Education and Science inspectors, approval was given, as from 1 September 1981, for any child in the United Kingdom who had been successfully auditioned for entry into Chetham's to be eligible for a central government grant.

Meanwhile there remained the problem of providing accommodation and practice-rooms as the number of resident pupils
increased. Originally there had been forty Blue Coat boys in
the College building, and when, in the nineteenth century,
there were one hundred boys, an additional dormitory was
added. In the grammar school period there were about seventy
boarders. In 1975 the number was ninety-two: it was to be one
hundred and sixty in 1978 and to reach one hundred and eighty
in 1982. No new building took place and the rooms were found
by a remarkable process of adaptation. It was made possible
by the lifting of the restriction on further investment in capital
expenditure and by a successful appeal for funds. A complete
restructuring of the Palatine Buildings took place and the
former Manchester Grammar School building was acquired
and adapted. At last, the years of transition could be said to
be over.

What kind of school had emerged? It is always difficult to
define a school, but Chetham's had reached a stage at which
it was possible to explain its new purpose in the light of experience gained since music had begun to be an integral part of
the school. Originally Chetham's had prepared boys for
apprenticeships so that they could learn a trade. Later, it had
provided stimulus for boys who were preparing, through a
grammar school education, for entry into the professions. Now
it had become a specialist music school, and John Vallins
described its purpose in these terms:

> Like any kind of education, it has its vocational aspect, which
> should be taken seriously, but the argument for good musical edu-
> cation is that children need to sing, that some of them will never
> express themselves fully unless they have the chance to learn an
> instrument. Some, with particular talent, will be stunted unless
> they spend several hours a day developing the finer skills of instru-
> mental playing. . . . We want to be exclusive only in the sense that
> we must exclude children who we think will be unhappy here, and
> children will be unhappy in a specialist school unless they really
> want and need to develop their skills, through much hard work,
> in association with other children of similar bent. . . . Once a child
> is accepted, he or she will join a school which we hope and intend
> should not feel too unlike many others. With us, to be musical is

to be normal. . . . 'Music' at Chetham's fills about one third of the pupils' timetable time. . . . No one should seek a place at a music school primarily in order to find a way to earning a good living. We are, of course, delighted when one of our past or present pupils scores a success on the public platform, or in a competition, but we are delighted too when one becomes a musical doctor or a primary school teacher. We hope that, whatever they become, a few years of musical education have enriched them.[5]

5 John Vallins, 'Music – a joy and a mission', *The Educationist* (autumn 1982).

CHAPTER 8

Audition and settling-in

When Chetham's was a Hospital School the daily routine could
be described as a repeated process uniformly observed. The
pattern slightly changed during the grammar school period,
but with the advent of music the mould was broken and variation rather than standardisation became typical. At the
centre was the old school, but there were now different layers
of experience dependent on age, sex, geographical area, and
what instrument was being played. Boys between the age of
seven and ten no longer waited in the yard on Easter Mondays
in the hope of being elected to a vacancy. Neither were eleven-
year-olds waiting to know whether they had passed the entrance examination. It was now a seven-year-old string player,
or an eight-year-old pianist, or an eleven-year-old wind player,
or a thirteen-year-old brass player, or a fourteen-year-old
guitarist, or a sixteen-year-old cellist who come for the first
time under the archway to have an audition. About three
hundred and fifty auditions were held in 1982. Previously, virtually all the boys had come from homes within daily travelling distance from the centre of Manchester, but now all areas
of the United Kingdom have children at Chetham's. How have
they been selected?

The audition is a way of discovering potential. 'The
Chetham's School of Music have developed a method of testing
which sets out to reveal children's musical resourcefulness and
creative responses, and is flexible enough to be adapted to suit
the experience and personality of individual children.'[1] This
second Gulbenkian Report also stressed the importance of
motivation as an essential factor in the selection process. Motivation cannot be measured, yet without it coping with the
demands of a specialist school, and a possible career later in
music, would be very hazardous. A regular visitor to the school

1 *Training Musicians: A Report to the Calouste Gulbenkian Foundation on the
training of professional musicians* (1978), p. 34.

has thoughtfully commented: 'As I've walked round the school, I found the children open and frank and easy, not children under stress. This says a lot about the selection process. These selected children are peculiar not only in their musical gift but in that most of them have stable, settled personalities, and they are open, spontaneous children. I wonder how much of this is necessary to be successful at music.'

Auditions seek much more than mere performance on an instrument. Each audition is different and so it is not possible to make a general statement about auditioning, but Michael Brewer has indicated some of the ways in which potential and motivation have been explored. 'Imitating on an instrument what is played on a piano; then moving to an answering phrase and, if they understand modulation, changing key and coming home again: and composing snippets of tune and variations on them. All this is done spontaneously, and what direction it takes depends on the individual child. There are very few who can get far, but with those who can respond well, that is the kind of child we're looking for. Ear tests are sometimes irrelevant because they can reflect a total lack of previous experience, or they can demonstrate that a child has been drilled precisely. We all know the situation in a junior school where someone has a musical talent and is likely to be the pianist in assembly but is never stretched beyond that. The dangerous thing can be that the child – and more particularly the family – exaggerate the musical ability. One advantage of the audition is that the ability can be looked at more realistically and that a child of exceptional talent can feel more normal by being with others of comparable ability.'

What does it feel like to be auditioned? The usual response is that after initial hesitation, the experience is enjoyable because of the opportunity being provided for the unexpected. 'I was very nervous', declared an eleven-year-old, 'but I didn't know it was going to be such fun.' A fourteen-year-old clarinettist had this comment to make: 'Demands are made on you which you've never experienced before. I had done simple aural things before, but he asked me to play the main theme of my piece up a tone from memory. To start with, I didn't know the piece from memory. Secondly I couldn't pick out the main theme. Thirdly, to transpose it was another thing entirely. But it wasn't too bad. Only when he pushed me did it get heavy going.' Often, the local authority music adviser is present at the audition, as well as an expert on the particular instrument.

A few singers are admitted through audition, but all the other pupils are instrumentalists. Performance on an instrument is therefore a prime essential, and this does raise a serious social question. To reach the standard necessary for consideration for audition, both an instrument and tuition on that instrument are needed. Instruments are expensive and, together with tuition, can be a heavy drain on parental income. Does this mean that Chetham's had become a school for the socially advantaged in that it can only provide for children whose families can afford instruments and tuition? A look at the way in which youngsters have come first to an instrument, and then later reached Chetham's does not support what this question implies.

A six-year-old in a primary school on the coast of Wales discovers a cello in the classroom. 'It was just a spare cello for anybody who would like to start. My family were not musical although we listened to records a lot. It was a quarter size cello, and once I started there were weekday lessons from a visiting teacher, paid for by the local authority. In time, I played at a festival and the adjudicators recommended that I should have an assessment. I was eleven by then, and played the Bourrée from the third Bach suite at my audition. It was a great shock coming from Wales to Manchester. I wish Chetham's was somewhere else, but I don't regret coming, because there is no other place. There was no other choice. I could have stayed where I was, but my cello teacher didn't think she could take me any further.'

In the North East, when violins were offered to children in a primary school for the first time an eight-year-old responded to the opportunity. Father had once played a clarinet, but the family was not musical in any professional sense. The instrument was now available and tuition followed. A successful audition for entry into Chetham's took place at the age of thirteen, but that year the local authority was unable to provide a grant. This was before 1981 when approval was given for families to receive grants from central government instead of local authorities. Without financial aid the family could not support the child at Chetham's, and it was not until a year later that the violinist came with a local authority grant. 'I expected it to be very plush, but it was quite tatty and homely. It's so much like being in a big family. Although you lose your friends at home, I've friends now in all sorts of different areas of the country, I'm not just restricted to my home town.'

There are other ways of encountering an instrument. 'Mum used to run a Sunday School and needed accompaniment for the hymn singing so she went to night-school to learn how to play a guitar. She brought music back with her. She taught me at first, but we had trouble in finding a proper teacher in our village in Derbyshire because I was so young. I was only ten. We were helped by music scholarships which paid for travelling expenses and for lessons. I first went to Derby for guitar lessons and then on to Nottingham. I had junior music scholarships from the age of ten until I was fourteen, when I came to Chetham's.'

Here were needs being recognised and supported by local authority finance. There have also been other sorts of need. A twelve-year-old boy, in care because the home circumstances were unsuitable, was sent to a special boarding-school for treatment for asthma and eczema and where, each day, there was a compulsory rest period at midday. To avoid boredom, he was given a violin to play with. He had had no previous experience of violin playing but his progress was so rapid that on return to his home-base the local authority arranged for an audition. Throughout his stay at Chetham's the local authority, not the family, provided boarding and tuition fees. His health record improved, he went on to music college and today he has a place in one of our professional orchestras. Another local authority arranged for an audition for a nine-year-old boy pianist who would have attended a school for the educationally sub-normal. Although his physical age was nine, his reading age was that of a five-year-old. The audition revealed his musical potential, and for the next ten years he was a pupil at Chetham's. Usual academic expectations were not possible, but that did not matter because the lack of academic ability was compensated for by his other strengths. He had the esteem of his peers because of his piano playing. He was a very caring boy with strong personal relationships. Although his effort never slackened and he was provided with remedial teaching, he was to leave the school without any 0 level grades. Orally he had much to communicate, particularly with regard to music and religion, but he had difficulty in expressing his thoughts on paper. Even so, the distinctive gift had been recognised and allowed to develop, and he was able to leave Chetham's for college as the next stage in preparation for a career in music.

These are exceptional examples. The usual pattern is for a child to be acceptable in other directions as in music. The question has been raised that children of lower academic ability should be excluded, that an IQ test be included in an audition, and that children below a score of one hundred and ten should not be admitted. The admission policy at Chetham's has remained unchanged. The audition is concerned solely with musical potential. Experience has shown that there exists a high correlation between musical and other abilities, and where, exceptionally, this is not so, provision can be made for remedial teaching, as would be the case in any other school with a comprehensive intake.

There still remains a difficulty in deciding at an early age whether a specialist school would be the most appropriate form of education for a particular child. Other countries have systems for classification and selection, but here much more depends on the family and the child. 'My music teacher did not say that I should go to Chetham's, but that it would be worth while to have an audition to see whether the experts thought I had any talent. I didn't really want to come at first because Chetham's would be so different to what I was used to. I wasn't sure whether I wanted to be a pianist when I grew up. We had a piano from my grandmother, but I was never forced to play. At the primary school I was the only one interested in music so I was always playing at concerts and accompanying at music practices. People treated me as if I were a pianist, but I was interested in so many things in the junior school that I wasn't sure what to make my mind up on. It was only after a second audition that I came round to the idea that the piano was becoming more important to me than anything else. Having now been at Chetham's for three years, I don't know what I was worried about. It was a sort of fear of the unknown that had made me hesitate.'

For one or two pupils, the usual audition would not be possible because they live overseas. In the light of strong recommendations they have been brought to the attention of the school, and after considering all the circumstances, a decision is made about entry. One such example was a fourteen-year-old boy in Cyprus who in his local school was concentrating on the natural sciences because he intended ultimately to study medicine at Athens University. He had violin lessons and his hobby was composing music. 'I used to lock myself in a room and write music for hours. One of my quartets was sent to the Ministry of Education at a time when they were looking for some music to represent Cyprus at an international children's festival at Sofia in Bulgaria. My music was chosen and played, and out of this came the suggestion that an application be made to Chetham's. The fact that Chetham's combined both music and a thorough teaching of academic subjects appealed to my parents because they wanted me to carry on with my academic work. The telegram announcing that I could come to Chetham's arrived only two weeks before the term started. I could hardly speak any English, although I had learned it as an examination subject.' He quickly settled down, with help mastered his English, continued, and reached good standards in his scientific studies, as well as developing his skills both as violinist and composer. The cost of his education was borne by his government and family, and after four years he went on to university to read music.

Children come from all quarters and backgrounds and seem to adapt quickly to the unusual conditions at Chetham's – buildings which have been, and still are being, adapted, an inner city environment which is not what would normally be expected for a boarding school, and pressures not only to reach high musical standards, but also high academic standards. Clearly there is an advantage in boarding because it provides total involvement in all that is taking place. Many children, however, have not come from families where there is a tradition of all the family having been in boarding schools. Basic skills such as learning how to wash themselves and doing their own hair have to be taught, and once they can do these for themselves settling-in is not difficult. Days are set aside in the summer term, while the school is in session, for the parents of newcomers to see for themselves how the school is run. The youngsters are matched up with youngsters of the same age, and, if possible, the same instrument, and they wander around together without their parents. In this frank and friendly way, new children form friendships and quickly get to know what time lights-out is, what the staff are like, etc.

On the resident side there are four Houses: a junior house for boys and girls between the ages of seven and twelve, a boys' house for thirteen to eighteens, and two girls' houses also for thirteen to eighteens. There is a fifth House for day-pupils, who form just under a quarter of the school population of about two hundred and forty, where the age range is from eight to eighteen. The difference between being a teacher on a daily basis and a teacher in charge of a house of about fifty pupils can sometimes be overlooked. The transition from being mostly a day grammar school for boys to becoming mostly a boarding coeducational school for young musicians has proved to be a learning situation for the teaching staff. 'Previously, I was a Head of Department, a full-time teacher and knew the children I taught, but only in the classroom. Now that I am in charge of a House, I have come to know them as people, as individuals. I was guilty as a younger teacher of treating them as if they were very special. In one sense they are, but the gift they have does not demand treating them in special ways as if they were freaks. They gave the same physical development as other children, the same emotional problems and the same family relationships. Girls find out about boys at the same time as any other child in the whole country. Our job is to make sure that their particular gift is developed, but on the other hand your relationship with them, the way you treat them, the disciplining hold you have over them, and the help you try to give them would be the same as in any school.'

And, of course, for resident staff it is a twenty-four-hour seven day commitment. 'If you join a boarding community you've got to enjoy it. You don't think of it as just a job – it's a way of life. You have to accept that term-time is wholly school time. We chop up our life into two clearly separate sections, term-time which is school, and holiday which is home.' One of the hardest things is to avoid being engulfed in term-time. 'It's like the plant that traps flies – the school keeps you here, but you know you've got to get out of the gates to keep a sense of perspective. You can't keep giving out and not putting anything back.'

The break with home can be traumatic, particularly at an early age, but it need not be if every care is taken to prepare the way beforehand. Such preparation was not always possible in the days when there could be a delay between a successful audition and approval for a grant. 'We didn't know that the local authority would make it possible for me to come until the Friday before term started. I was having nightmares. My dreams would start off with heads of me going down a conveyor belt into a huge black hole, and as the nights progressed, they turned into torsos, and then the whole me. My first night is vividly etched in my mind. It seemed as if I were never to go home again. I was a weekly boarder, but going home at weekends was so unsettling that I never stayed a full week until I had the courage to become a full boarder. Maybe I was playing a game and trying to see how far I could push my parents to see if they really would take me away. But after the first full week of boarding, I settled in and have never since looked back.'

It is possible both to exaggerate and to minimize the initial impact of boarding. After the first week or so, experience has shown that settling in presents little difficulty, largely because of the involvement in music. Every three weeks there are 'free weekends' when boarders are encouraged to return home or stay with friends. These are weekends free from Saturday morning full orchestral tuition, a break considered necessary because of the intensity of music-making and the claustrophobic effect of being in an inner-city area where on weekdays there are busy shops and office-blocks but very few people at weekends. Quite apart from the impossible cost of removing the school to a more open area, the advantages of being at the centre of Manchester, near the Hallé and BBC Philharmonic orchestras and the Royal Northern College of Music, and near railway stations, far outweigh the benefit of having more space but being remote. Even so, there remains the hesitation about boarding: 'Although it would be an advantage to board, it would mean growing up quicker than you would normally. When you are at home, you think of leaving when you are eighteen, but if you board you would be cutting out a third of your childhood.' And from a boarder: 'I keep in close touch with my family, but I'm also close to lots of people here. I've got two lives really and the two of them are connected by music. Being away from home makes you feel independent. Being independent is all right provided it doesn't make you want to break away from anything else.'

Occasionally a day-pupil has become a boarder on progressing through the school:

I was very happy at the comprehensive school but Chetham's gave me what wasn't available elsewhere. I was a twelve-year-old girl playing in a military band. There was only one of me and there were twelve clarinets, and I had to overblow to be heard, which is not good for an oboist. I would have liked to have come earlier than when I was fourteen, but the government grant scheme was only put into operation the year I came, so I wouldn't have been able to come any earlier anyway. When I was a day pupil I would get up at 6.45 and travel by train to be in time for the 8.30 start to the day. When I became involved in a wind quintet, lessons and practice together would keep me at school for three nights in the week when I would be catching the 9.30 train back home. This was in my O level year and since then I've become a boarder so that I can benefit from full participation. I am very glad that I went to a comprehensive school first because it makes me appreciate both sides of the education system.

It is interesting to learn how Chetham's appears to pupils with previous experience of a different kind of education.

You'd go into a choir and he would say: 'Sing a G major chord'. No piano would be sounded, and people with perfect pitch would start a G major chord. He would say 'up or down' a tone and you just did it. That was fantastic for me, because I'd come from a school where we had to sit and learn the notes by imitation. I had been frustrated at school because although the school was academically very good and I enjoyed that part of it, musically it was so unsatisfactory. It was good to be in a place where other people were good at the same thing. What really hit me was to find that there were people better than me. It was much better to know when I was fifteen that I wasn't half as good as I thought I was, rather than wait until I went to a university to find that out. For me, actually to say: 'I'm not good enough' is quite something. I don't think I could even have said that if I hadn't been to Chetham's.

Personal statements of this nature may seem slightly dramatic, but adolescence is a time of drama, a discovery of individuality. 'It was my first time away from home and I was sixteen. Suddenly finding myself among people of my own age, I went a bit wild. It was so euphoric to be given all this freedom, being in a big city with people who were so interesting and interested in the sort of things I liked. It seemed so new then, but in fact we were only really continuing our education, not starting anything new. We were still at school. After a year I wondered whether I wanted to spend the rest of my life among musicians. When I was at home I was led to expect that because I was the best there it would be easy to continue in music for the rest of my life. If you're not suited for a music career, you find out at Chetham's. That is one of the important things that Chetham's taught me.' Another senior pupil also called attention to a sense of freedom which came from being among musicians. 'At my other school, it was a place you went to for five hours during the day. You kept yourself to yourself if your interests were not the same as others. Music was considered an improper and precarious profession. When you come to Chetham's the comparative freedom – musically, intellectually, socially – is a big thing happening all at once. It is something to do with freedom not in the sense of doing forbidden things, but in the sense of actually being yourself in an environment with similar people. The sharing of a common language of music is a sort of freedom.'

Relaxation

A new bedroom in the Palatine Building

Wind trio with Lady Barbirolli

Brass master-class with Philip Jones

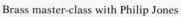

Gerald Littlewood conducting the school orchestra in the dormitories.
Duchess of Kent's visit, 1970

A rehearsal in the new Studio, opened 1981

CHAPTER 9

Music School

It is generally acknowledged that the methods formulated by Zoltán Kodály have produced remarkable results in developing musicianship among school children. But, as the second Gulbenkian Report (1978) pointed out: 'The real problem is that the Kodály method requires teachers who are both excellent musicians (and these are by no means common in primary schools) and who have been specially trained in the appropriate teaching methods. It also assumes a continuity throughout the primary school, rarely found in music in British schools.'[1] Teachers with experience of the Kodály method in Hungary are at present teaching at Chetham's, and although the method is not followed in all its strict detail, the basic principles are observed. The teaching of music at Chetham's begins, therefore, with the training of the inner ear.

All pupils in the seven to twelve age-group meet in classes for hourly sessions on Mondays, Wednesdays and Friday. The singing momentum is also maintained with choir training on Tuesdays and Thursdays. Thus, five hours in the week are devoted to ear training. Michael Brewer has commented: 'Individually the work they do derives from inner listening. The best way to express inner listening is to sing because that is your natural instrument. The more you are involved, both in aural training and in academic music, in singing, the more the capacity to hear music will develop. You would actually be hearing tunes inside your head without them being played. Also, you would be hearing in advance before you play the sounds on your instrument.'

This is not a revolutionary approach to musical education but is different from the usual emphasis placed on first learning an instrument as a means of introducing young people to music. One of the teachers has explained the difference as follows: 'When we set about learning an instrument in our

1 Appendix C, *Training Musicians* (1978), p. 134.

youth we are doing several things at the same time. We are not only learning to use fingers and arms in a way we haven't done before, but at the same time we are learning to read a new language. Inner hearing is as important to a musician as the mind's eye is to an artist. A musician has to respond to the mind's ear. Unfortunately, a tradition of music teaching has come to be based on the eye. Through the Kodály approach to teaching and the training of the inner hearing, we are trying to enable children to imagine how a piece of music sounds when they see it.'

The approach, then, is less visual, and less muscular, and the concentration is on accuracy and response to listening. It is also less theoretical in the initial stages. The first Gulbenkian Report (1965) had drawn attention to the complexity of a theoretical approach to music.[2] The Kodály method is a means of avoiding the difficulties that arise from too early a stress on theory. 'At first there should be no reading or writing. Most things will have to be learned by rote from the teacher who actually does the singing as well, rather than playing the piano. A wide repertoire of all sorts of songs – slow songs, low songs, high songs, loud songs, soft songs – is built up so that later, while that repertoire is being extended, the teacher can gradually bring in the theoretical training based on what has earlier been experienced. Without that experience it would be like teaching reading to a child who does not have conversations with parents and who has not been read to by parents. Children are being involved in a practical musical experience rather than being confronted with a theoretical and intellectualised aspect of music.'

2 'The young music-student, whether instrumental or vocal, has to master a new language with a new alphabet of considerable complexity (different clefs, marks of expression, key signatures, etc.) none of which is ambiguous; and this makes for accuracy. He must learn this language swiftly and with ease, bearing many factors (e.g. key and time-signatures, accidentals) in mind over a long period; and he must "translate" what he reads with lightning speed into action, i.e. sounds, produced either by the voice, the fingers or a difficult combination of arm-and-finger (strings) or breath-and-finger (wind) movements. This is an unrivalled school of memory-training and mental-physical coordination. The music that he sings or plays gives, according to its nature, either an acquaintance with the principle of abstract thought ("thinking in sound") or an experience of emotional expression on the highest level; in the greatest music these two are combined' (p. 28).

The electronic age has brought recorded music and tape-recording into schools. While welcome as a means to an end, music appreciation in itself is not a suitable way of teaching without prior practical experience. Even where classroom instruments such as the glockenspiel and xylophone are available and popular, there is the drawback of training the muscular movement of finger and arm and approaching music in a physical way, not through the voice and the ear. One teacher had commented: 'Although I previously taught in a school which seemed to have success in parental or schoolmasterly terms because end-of-term concerts were good, for the vast majority of children in that school music had little significance. The concerts were given by the few hand-picked children, the top of the pyramid. You went through the usual hoops of teaching through lines, spaces and clefs, which are meaningless to children who do not play instruments. Music teachers themselves, through no fault of their own, had come to read and play music by a one-to-one relationship with an instrumental teacher, which is not a satisfactory preparation for teaching at least thirty in a class. The experience in Hungary was quite different. What was so impressive was the total involvement of large groups of children, and the sense of enjoyment, not only on the part of the teacher but also by all the pupils. The achievement levels are high and are directed at all children.'

It would be expected for a music school to have a broader music syllabus than that laid down by examination boards. A two-year foundation course after the age of twelve is being developed at Chetham's, with the purpose of strengthening and broadening general musicianship. Two hours each week are devoted to the course which is examinable two years later. The way is thereby prepared for A level at the end of Lower Sixth, leaving the final year for greater scope for instrumental work and any specialist interest. It is hoped that exchange visits abroad might be arranged during the final year without risk of missing out on an academic qualification.

Cathedral choristers are part of the school, but retain their independence as a choir school annexed to Chetham's. When the school was passing through its transitional period, the distinction was not so clearly defined. There had been a previous arrangement whereby a chorister could continue with his education at Chetham's after his voice had broken. As the school became more specialised, a former chorister would not be at home with what the rest of the school was absorbed in unless he himself was an instrumentalist. Take an example from 1977, when a chorister wanted to leave the choir before his voice broke in order to become an instrumentalist. The Cathedral had expected to retain his full experience until his voice broke, and if other members were to be allowed to leave, it would be difficult to maintain a choir at the Cathedral. It became necessary to differentiate between choristers who were given places in the school and instrumentalists selected to the school by audition. The boy was informed, 'Being a chorister is considered a particular and positive role within the Chetham community, and the chorister commitment when undertaken implies that until the chorister's voice breaks singing in the choir is his single and most important activity within the school'.

It so happened that this particular boy served his full term as chorister, was able to qualify as an instrumentalist, and ultimately left Chetham's with a university organ-scholarship. He was glad to have had the situation clarified for him: 'Do not get the impression that I bear any grudge for not being allowed to leave the choir. It is much fairer to know exactly where you stand. A chorister commitment is a full commitment. When you are in the Cathedral choir you have to concentrate on singing. It becomes your life. When your voice breaks, it is fair to have a re-audition for an instrument if you want to stay at Chetham's, otherwise it would not be an appropriate education. The difficulty had arisen in my time because some choristers had been allowed to stay on, and they had become outsiders.'

A chorister's commitment is a considerable one, with Evensong on Tuesdays, Thursdays and Saturdays and two services on Sunday. If a boy is a talented string player or pianist, he would find it difficult to fit in enough instrumental practice as well as rehearsing and singing at the Cathedral. It may seem a harsh decision that a boy's schooling may have to change at, say, the age of thirteen when his voice breaks, but he would be better served in a different school unless his music potential, as evidenced by another audition, would suit him for Chetham's. Both the Master of the Cathedral Choir and the Cathedral Organist teach at Chetham's, and every care is taken to ensure that both musical and academic work are at a level which would make possible a suitable transfer to another school.

All the choristers are day-pupils and live within travelling distance from the school. Inside the school, the day begins at 7.00 a.m. In the Blue Coat days, it had been 6.00 a.m., followed by trades and a breakfast at 8.00 a.m. Trades are still carried out but in a very modified form. There are no fires to stoke up or cobbled pathways to sweep, but there are rooms to tidy and laundry to collect and transport. Twelve-year-olds are the supervisors in the junior House and breakfast is at 7.30 a.m. Practice begins at 8.00 a.m. Possibly the most difficult adjustment that a junior has to face is to practise in a strange room on his own for the first time, without a mother or father to encourage and advise. Experience has shown that in a very short time a warm rapport develops with the practice supervisor and that is because she is so much more than a music guide. The trust and loving care manifests itself in many ways, as can be illustrated by the following incident. A seven-year-old boy is upset when he reaches his practice room, not because of his music, but because older boys in his dormitory had played football with his teddy bear, his link with his home. The teddy bear's ear is damaged. It would have been easy, and might have seemed sensible, to tell the boy not to be such a baby and get on with his practice. What happened was different, and reveals the trust that was developing, as well as the deep sense of loneliness in the child. 'I'll mend the ear,' said the supervisor. There was a pause. 'Will you? When?' Not straightaway, the supervisor explained, because she did not have a needle and thread available. 'I'll take teddy home with me and bring him back tomorrow with his ear mended.' Another pause. 'Will you take him to bed with you?' The answer was: 'Of course.' There was a deep sign of relief, the face brightened and practice could now begin. 'You see,' the youngster said, 'he has never slept on his own before.'

Practice time varies for different age groups, and supervisors are available from 8.00 a.m. until 10.00 p.m. For instrumentalists under the age of eleven, there is an expectation of two hours practice each day, with possibly less for wind and brass players. From the age of eleven to thirteen, an average of two and a half hours a day is expected, while for older pupils the time is extended to four hours each day, with a degree of variation dependent on the number of O and A level examinations being undertaken. This may sound very much like regimentation. One former pupil, now a distinguished pianist, put it this way: 'It is important that there should be free time to practise. It is very difficult to know whether you can force people to practise. I think they have to have the freedom to do so when they wish. If they don't have their own motivation to practise, they are not going to have it. It is something that comes very much from within themselves.' This is very true. Practice does continue outside the set times, but for as many as two hundred and forty pupils and with limited facilities, a system of set times is a necessity for regular daily practice to take place at all. Unless special provision were made, there would be tremendous frustration and disappointment. Even with the recent addition of forty-seven practice-rooms, there are still times when extra space is needed. There is need for a framework, but it is only a framework. As Walter Giesekind is reported as saying: 'Virtuosity is a mental process, not a matter of practising hour after hour.'

Each pupil has two lessons each week in their first study instrument and one in second study. The academic day begins at 8.30 a.m. and ends at 4.30 p.m., but instrumental tuition takes place outside these limits as well as within them. Each child has a timetable which varies according to the availability of tutors, but no child is withdrawn from an academic lesson unless exceptional circumstances have arisen. There are three categories among the eighty visiting tutors. There are those who are home-based in the Manchester area who can provide a regular weekly schedule. There are others who are professionally engaged in orchestras such as the BBC Philharmonic and the Hallé and whose tutorial time is directed by the demands of their orchestra. Such established orchestras work according to a regular pattern so that weekly tuition can be planned, although times might occasionally vary. The third category is the free-lance orchestral player, usually from London, who may also be pursuing an international career. It is regarded as essential that the more advanced pupils should benefit from the breadth of musical and technical experience which such tutors can provide, even though there may not always be regular weekly lessons.

With so many teachers visiting the school, there could be fragmentation, but the general sense of purpose overrides all else, and with the passage of time, the disparity between academic and music staff has considerably lessened. There are bound to be differences of emphasis because an academic world and the world of the professional musician are two very different places. Whatever glamour may have coloured the expectations of youngsters, the regular contact with practising musicians on a one-to-one basis produces a realistic approach to a career in music. 'It is a big mistake to let people go into the music profession feeling they are special in some way,' says one tutor who has been associated with Chetham's for over twenty years. 'There is nothing special about the profession except that it is selective, it is small, and it is merciless on any shortfall in standards. To go in with too great an idea of your own ability is about the worst mistake you can make. Sometimes young string players are wrongly encouraged with the idea that they would be disappointed with themselves if they played in an orchestra. You have to have the completest kind of education. Walk into any orchestral bandroom and you'll find people who are linguists, historians, who have degrees in law or the sciences. It is not correct to suppose that excellence in music is exclusive of all other things. Indeed the other things tend to help the music eventually. The profession is both physically and mentally demanding, much beyond the level which would seem to be apparent from watching players play either on television or on the concert platform.'

Preparation for a career in music can be very demanding, so demanding that the question could be raised as to whether excessive pressure is being exerted on children at too early an age. If there were a similar school in the United Kingdom with which comparison could be made, perhaps a clearer picture would be possible. As it is, Chetham's is unique in admitting children solely by audition and providing tuition in all instruments of the orchestra, as well as a general academic education. Is the school too career-orientated? The question was put to a visiting tutor:

Obviously one cannot be certain, up to say the age of fourteen or fifteen, whether a child will eventually want a career in music, however gifted a child may be or however much he or she may want to be a performer. It would be quite wrong, as it were, to force a decision. But one thing is certain, and this is the unfortunate part of it, that if you don't behave as if he were going to be a performer, by that age the door will more or less effectively have been closed, because the groundwork will not have been sufficiently prepared. From that point of view we have to behave as if the intention was there. What is apparently lost if he or she then decides not to continue with music is very little in comparison with what has been gained. They have been learning to work in a very concentrated way. I am sceptical when some educationists say that it is wrong to subject children to vocational training at an early age. I do not think that they are losing their childhood as a result. One of the reasons that I teach in a school like this is because of a sentence at the beginning of Thomas Mann's *The Magic Mountain*: 'We do not fear being called meticulous, inclining as we do to the view that only the exhaustive can be truly interesting'. I think that exploration of depth at any age is an educational experience.

It is interesting to speculate on why teachers teach at Chetham's, particularly those living busy professional lives who have to travel considerable distances to reach the school 'One learns how to handle this sort of situation. For me the train journey is very essential because that is the only time I can do my correspondence. I have no other time.' Another, who has visited for a number of years: 'The number of gifted children when I first came was not that high, but now it is enormous. We've probably got the most remarkable concentrated collection of musically gifted children under one roof that must exist almost anywhere outside Eastern European states or America.' Or a teacher in charge of physical education. 'It's the challenge! In the grammar school days it was easy to pick fifteen boys and coach them, because they wanted to learn. A musical child can spend so much time on musical skills that there is little time left for learning other skills. Many lack ball skills and some cannnot swim. We have to devise a means whereby children do not get injured and yet learn body awareness. By learning body awareness, you understand yourself, and when you understand yourself, you can perform better. For example, if you can overcome the fear of water, you become a stronger person within yourself. I see the opportunities being given to the children, and my job is to help them as much as possible. I take my job not so much as a job but as a part of my life.'

As for pupils, being with others who share similar musical experience and aspiration has produced a common sense of purpose which strengthens the sense of community. 'When I began to help at Chetham's, I had expected there to be a lot of emotional instability and hysterical behaviour because I suspected that the children were under considerable pressure to succeed, and that great demands were being made of them because they were expected to reach a high standard in music and quite a high standard academically. But this did not turn out to be the case. I was aware, of course, from some children, that there was a fair amount of jealousy about promotion in music, but they seemed to adjust to it. I welcomed the quality of openness and being willing to talk freely about themselves. I think I would define it as a normal open relationship from an uncomplicated child who is not under a great deal of stress, or at least can tolerate the stress they are under.'

Pupils who lived through the changes as the school became more musical occasionally had mixed feelings about the encroachment of the specialisation. 'Although music means so much to me, otherwise I wouldn't be here, I have too many other interests and I wouldn't want to sacrifice them totally. Music just comes like breathing, you take it for granted. It's been a driving force to play music but not to earn my living by music. That is why I chose science A levels. I would be completely demoralised if I started now. A young child of seven suddenly thrust into an environment such as this when so much is concentrated on music would make you think that your only aim in life was to be a musician. That is a very daunting prospect. For those who know at the age of seven that they are going to be a violinist, it is marvellous, but I don't think that all children do!'

Individual choice of career depends on a number of factors in addition to a talent in music – home background, the personality of the pupil, the influence of teachers and peers, academic qualifications, even the impact of adolescence. There have been pupils who were admitted solely on musical potential who have demonstrated exceptional ability in other directions as well, and have left Chetham's to read other subjects than music at universities. Attention is given to all aspects of a child's development, not merely the musical element, and care is taken to ensure that when options have to be taken after the first two foundation years in the senior school, it is the total child's potential that is being considered.

When I came in 1969 the possibility of a career in music was openly talked about. By the age of fourteen I had obtained the highest piano mark in England for Grade VIII of the Associated Board examinations. The curriculum at Chetham's gave me the advantage of being able to choose the sciences without any pressure being exerted on me. It was my own decision. I had to weigh up what I wanted to do and I decided that if I were a musician I couldn't be an amateur scientist, whereas if I were a scientist I could be an amateur musician. My parents may have felt disappointed, but they realised that I had ability in both, so they supported me when I changed direction. I don't feel the school ever discouraged me from going in a scientific direction, although when I was taking the Performers' Diploma there was an incredible amount of time-pressure on me to do enough practice. In the comprehensive school in which I now teach science, music is just as essential as more utilitarian subjects such as English language and mathematics. We need art forms to express ourselves and share experience, and music is the highest and most accessible art form there is. I do not regret the decision I made.

Competitons have become an increasingly important part of the preparation for launching a career as a soloist. One such development has been the BBC 'Young Musician of the Year' for under-eighteen-year-olds who have gained a Grade VIII distinction in the Associated Board examination. In the first competition in 1978, one Chetham's pupil was joint winner in the piano class, and another was second in the woodwind class. Both have since been able to follow successful careers as soloists. In the second competition in 1980 a Chetham's pupil was third in the string class and became a section finalist in the next competition two years later. He was accompanied by two other Chetham's pupils as section finalists in 1982, and it was the piano finalist who won the title. For the school, musical competition of this kind has to be placed in an educational context. Experience has shown that the challenge can bring out of their performance something far better than the performers had previously thought themselves capable of. Yet there are reservations. The publicity, and the emphasis on simply being the winner rather than playing well could unbalance a young person's approach. There is also over-exposure to the pressures that come with early success. One of the pressures is the risk of not having sufficient repertoire. It can happen that within one season there is not enough to continue the success with, so concerts are not offered, and the next competition winners take over. In the school situation there is the danger of over-strain and of possible damage to the general and academic curriculum if too much time and energy were to be devoted to competition. In the run-up to the 1982 competition came this cry from the heart: 'I apologise for the appalling content of this essay. I do not like to say that I have been 'under pressure' recently since I consider this to be a feeble excuse for not doing work properly. I will be OK once I get myself sorted out. The trouble is that I've got so much to live up to: it's really horrible wondering whether you're going to be ready for the next concert or exam, but although I moan and grouse, I would hate to do anything else. I just hate doing badly, and so if I can do this essay properly later and to the best of my ability, please could I do it?' Needless to say, the request was granted, the competition was won and academic success followed as well.

There has to be a degree of competitiveness within the school itself. 'If you don't get in the first two desks you feel a complete failure. It is good to a certain extent to have competition which is needed to get on, but only to a certain extent. I do not know whether there is any other way. Music itself matters, not the competitiveness.' A different pupil added: 'The day that orchestra lists would go up, there were tears all over the place. Looking back, it was the best way to do it. Orchestral auditions were carried out fairly and only the best should be in the orchestra. If you're not as good as others, you shouldn't be allowed to think you are.' There is the premonition here of the selection process which is an inescapable part of a musical career. A visiting tutor has this to say:

> From child to child the pressure is different. Some will be able to take it, some will not. Competition is necessary so that a pupil will do his or her best. To be too comfortable is not part of our life. Unfortunately, agents and managers in the profession are there to get as much money out of a talent as possible. If the talent gets exhausted, nobody cares. They are thrown out and the next one is taken in. There can be a lot of unfair competition where musicians are just being used as a means of making money. Children need to be taught how to manage themselves in the difficult circumstances outside the school. Music, being very much a minority interest, is very competitive.

Naturally, in a specialist music school, the involvement of all children in performance is of prime consideration. With four choirs, three orchestras, some ensemble groups and two hundred and forty instrumentalists, the problem is how to provide sufficient time without trespassing too much on academic work. Each year a programme of major concerts is drawn up, not all centred on Manchester but including areas from which pupils have come. There are also composers' concerts when work done by pupils receive a first performance, and conductors' concerts in which pupils gain experience of conducting. But the main contribution to performing experience comes with regular lunch-time concerts, and the three major concerts usually prepared for after a week when academic work is relaxed. In 1982 there were eighty-nine lunch-time concerts, and even in the summer term, when academic pressure was at its highest with O and A level external examinations, there were one hundred and eight pupils being given the opportunity to perform in public. Standards are high because no performance can take place without the approval of tutors. The instrumental range and the number of players in each category during the summer term were: flute (4), oboe (4), clarinet (4), bassoon (1), recorder (1), trumpet (3), violin (12), viola (5) cello (13), singing (8), piano (26), accompaniment (20), harpsichord (1) and ensemble (84). In 1983 the summer concert at the Free Trade Hall, Manchester, as part of the Hallé Promenade Season, involved fifty-two pupils in the senior orchestra and ninety-nine pupils in two choirs. The programme consisted of: Bach, Cantata No. 50; Schütz, *German Magnificat*; Saint-Saëns, *Carnival of the Animals*; Rachmaninov, *Rhapsody on a Theme of Paganini*; Stravinsky, *The Firebird Suite* (1919 version).

With so much concert preparation and participation, the question arises, particularly among the academic staff, as to whether too much attention is given to performance. Even among music tutors, there could be reservations: 'There is a need for time to develop basic skills. If a child is with this orchestra or with that orchestra, or in this concert or that concert, there can be too many demands. Children can be pulled in too many directions. Fewer concerts would give more time for the spade work.' On the other hand, a different emphasis could be stressed. 'It is one thing to work on details in a piece of music, another thing to present it in public. Even very top performers will not play for the first time a programme they are preparing for a major concert hall. They will try the programme out maybe a dozen times until it matures, and they are able to to view it from every angle. If a child is getting more used to performing, being familiar with the conditions of performing will enable that child to be more ready at a later stage.'

Where, then, should the line be drawn? What should be the appropriate balance between academic work and the music specialism? Such a question has had to be faced ever since music has been developing at Chetham's. At the centre is the musically gifted child, but around that child are many well-meaning but sometimes contradictory influences. Presiding over this creative friction are the Headmaster, John Vallins, and the Director of Music, Michael Brewer, and in 1982 a document was produced which described the overall view of Chetham's at the end of the transitional period which began in 1969. The year 1982 is regarded as a watershed because it was the first year in which full recognition by central government was operative. The following extracts define the place of the school in the education world.

> The School's particular responsiblility, to the Department of Education and Science and to its potential pupils, is to provide an education specifically devised for children with particular musical gifts and the motivation to develop them.
>
> The first purpose of our specialist training is to fulfil the human potential of the children in our care. To see it in any other light (as, for instance, primarily a means of equipping them to earn a living) is to have a false basis for arriving at a view of the right priorities for buildings, curriculum, timetable or staffing within the School. Some of our misunderstandings have stemmed from the view that what goes under the heading of music is all 'training', in the sense of narrow, imposed, physical discipline, whereas at Chetham's, uniquely, it is a peculiarly rich, full and varied educational experience.
>
> Another element is that by accepting children of different ages and from many different kinds of schools, we should be equipped and disposed to meet individual needs – musical, social, academic. If we seek to start from the point of the individual's needs and aspirations, we shall be wary of imposing in too totalitarian a way any one pattern of life or work.
>
> A third element is the idea that a decision to come to Chetham's does not imply a decision to become a professional, performing musician. It follows that the range and quality of academic work must be such as to enable children to enter universities and other courses in a sufficient range of subjects.
>
> A fourth element is the idea that the school should discourage pupils from feeling too isolated from the world at large, too superior, or from becoming too self-centred.
>
> It is the responsibility of the School's central administration to set the overall direction, to create space and opportunity for the initiative of teachers and pupils to make things happen.

CHAPTER 10

Specialism

We are not a specialist nation by habit. Some would say that the habit has been to select by social class rather than by ability. In Britain an impression has long persisted that in music we rely on gifted amateurs. A 'conservatoire' has a foreign flavour whereas a 'college' is so much more homely. In consequence, a specialist music school inherits the mantle of being only for the odd few taken out of the mainstream, a curiosity to be tolerated rather than a place serving a national need. The Plowden Report of 1967 drew attention to this problem.

> While it is universally admitted that exceptionally gifted people do exist, both the identification of them as children and the treatment that such children need are a matter of some disagreement. There is first of all what may be described as an egalitarian suspicion of the whole concept of giftedness. This is no less strong for being a mixture of, among other things, dislike of privilege, doubts about intelligence tests and defensiveness about comprehensive schools. At the outset giftedness meets with an irrational obstacle.... The general conclusion to be drawn is sufficiently obvious. The needs of the highly gifted, however we define them, must be met.... A possible solution is to concentrate them in certain schools... Music and ballet, for example, are difficult to provide at a high enough level except in a school staffed and equipped for the purpose. It must of course provide balance of education as well.

Ten years later, a working party of H.M. Inspectors reported on *Gifted Children in Middle and Comprehensive Schools*. They warned that it was a mistake to assume that 'the gifted can look after themselves', and added that it was also a mistake to think that 'to make provision for the exceptional is to do so at the expense of the unexceptional'. The case was put that because schools could not make provision from their own resources for educating the gifted child 'we look first at the possibility for provision by other institutions or agencies.... There are schools which exist as institutions for those with special gifts (for example in music and drama).'

This was the background as Chetham's was developing the resources for the education of musical children, but at a cost which rose rapidly in the 1970s. Such highly-skilled tuition, involving one-to-one lessons per child per week, as well as providing practice facilities, chamber music and orchestral training, brought the cost well above what would be considered a norm in education. Local Education Authorities came forward with support, but in the late 1970s, as money became tighter in education, it became harder to get discretionary grants. The survival of the school was made possible by the grant of fee-remission by the Department of Education and Science in 1981. Under Section 100 of the 1944 Education Act, which is applicable only to schools that specialise in the performing arts, parental contribution was calculated according to income. Since 1982 no child offered admission has been prevented by financial problems from joining, which had not always been the case previously.

Of the one hundred and ten entrants in 1983 and 1984, all government supported, fifteen came from independent schools and ninety-five from maintained schools. The social mix naturally reflects such cultural forces as home background, the availability of instruments and family income. The fee-remission scheme has made it possible for more opportunities to be available from maintained schools, and as the scheme becomes more widely known, the social range will be even wider. One interesting observation to make in the light of entries during these two years is the classification, accidental or otherwise, of instruments with areas. Among the string players, twenty-five per cent came from the southern counties with fifteen per cent from independent schools, while among brass players, none at all came from the south and none came from independent schools!

Before the specialism, when entry was by academic and non-musical examination, the situation was very different. Boys who had passed the eleven-plus examination could come with the local authority support, although numbers were restricted. Peter Donohoe, the distinguished pianist, awarded the joint Silver Prize at the Moscow International Tchaikovsky Piano Competition in 1982, came to the school in 1964 and spent the next seven years at Chetham's. His account throws light on the situation then for the recognition and development of exceptional ability.

> I did not come from a very musical family. We had a piano, my mother played a little, but I was already playing the piano at an advanced stage when I was young. It was a teacher in the state primary school who suggested that I should apply to Chetham's. My parents took the teacher's word for it, because they were not knowledgeable about reasons for selecting a particular grammar school. Although I didn't realise it at the time, I didn't fit in with the general class level of the rest of the school. Chetham's then had the image of a public school, not an ordinary school, and so far as I was concerned I was but one of two people in my form who were not being paid for by our parents, and we knew it. I had been reading stories about public schools and wanted to be part of one. All the years I was there I regretted not being a resident. I really did want to be one of the hard core, but we lived four miles away and we couldn't afford to pay the extra fees.

He played the third Beethoven piano concerto at the age of twelve with the school orchestra. His natural musical gift was sufficiently known at an early age for him to be regarded as a prodigy, but he was not required to specialise to the neglect of his general education.

> I was fortunate in my piano teacher, Donald Clarke, who was Head of the Science Department at Chetham's. His approach was very analytical, not only in a physical sense but also in finding out why a particular musical approach was not working. He would explain why that approach was a failure and suggest an alternative.
>
> My many successes have been gradual and never too early, and I am grateful for that. You could say that perhaps I was a child prodigy, but I did not go the way of a traditional child prodigy. My experience broadened at Chetham's, studying percussion equally with piano, and I continued with both to Diploma standard at the Royal Northern College of Music. When you leave college, there is no way you can walk into a career as a soloist. The mistake is to think solely of success as a soloist. David Oistrakh and Sviatoslav Richter started out as orchestral players, and in Richter's case as répétiteur and conductor as well. It should be encouraged in schools and colleges that to become a chamber-music player is not to become a second-class soloist, and to become an orchestral player is not to be a failure. Anyone who takes to music as a child

can easily be taken in by the glamour that surrounds a performer. The concert image takes over, and competitions contribute to the process. My advice to young pianists would be to get the stars out of their eyes, seize every opportunity to become involved in all aspects of music-making, and don't just concentrate on the instrument to the exclusion of all else. The opportunities at Chetham's have consider ably widened since I was there, so get involved.

When, after 1969, a larger number of local authorities undertook the financing either in part or in full of children at Chetham's, the strain on many parents was still considerable. Anna Markland, who was to be the BBC Young Musician of the Year in 1982, came to Chetham's in 1974 at the age of ten. It was a struggle for her parents to meet the costs, and the family is grateful for the ways in which Chetham's itself was able to help. Details are recalled, seemingly trivial, but they reflect the social difficulties of that time.

When my parents realised that I had to start wearing glasses, that was another aspect of the financial strain. They couldn't afford to buy private frames so I had to have National Health ones. I felt such a freak wearing them because they were different from the others. Children are sensitive about such things at that age. School uniform also put pressure on my parents because it was so expensive. We were glad to buy second-hand blouses and skirts which were on sale at the school. But I'm not against school uniform. When I was a prefect there was a move to try and abolish uniform in the sixth form but I opposed it. It is very important for a school to have an identity. If you belong to a school, you should be proud of what you belong to. Also, training for a musician is a discipline, and you need to be disciplined in other areas of your life.

The BBC competition is an example of the prematurely early success against which Peter Donohoe earlier gave a warning. Anna has seen it rather differently.

When I entered the competition, I wasn't clear in my mind that I was going to be a performer. I remember thinking that everybody else was going in for it, so why don't I have a go. I didn't rate my chances high, but I thought it would be a good way to extend my repertoire. My teacher encouraged me because she thought, unlike me, that I would do well. I never had much confidence in myself because other pianists always drew more attention than I did. Then there were the A level pressures. Also, I've been quoted as saying:

'A rift with a boy friend does wonders for playing Beethoven', and that was very true. However, I've no regrets because I'm proud of winning for my Mum and Dad. I'm so pleased for them and because pleasure is being given to so many people. I think my vocation in life is probably going to be on those lines.

There is danger in judging a school only by the success of pupils who have hit the headlines, and in any case Chetham's is so recently developed as a specialist school that it is too soon to be able to assess the long-term effects of the education it provides. The importance of a general education, however, should not be overlooked as the specialism has developed. In 1985 five pupils were admitted to universities to read subjects other than music – namely applied biology, chemistry, English, French and Russian. In that year, forty-four pupils completed the secondary stage of their education of whom thirty three went on to colleges and universities for further music study. It would seem that about eighty per-cent continue with music and will qualify as performers, orchestral players, teachers, composers, musicologists, even members of pop groups, as well as working in the recording or media industry. They were helped in 1985 by the award of eleven music scholarships, three for string players and two each for voice, piano, wind and brass. For those who would be seeking careers elsewhere than music their musical experience at Chetham's will be part of their lives and, as many letters from former pupils reveal, an important contribution to the community where they are living.

The reports dealing with specialist schools – the two Gulbenkian Reports of 1965 and 1978, the Plowden Report of 1970, the Inspectorate Report on *Gifted Children* of 1977 – emphasize the need to maintain a general education, and this Chetham's has done. The original fears that there would be a decline in academic standards have not been realised. The reverse has taken place, for academic standards have improved in spite of admission being solely by audition without any academic testing. It is as if the recognition and development of the special ability rubs off in other areas so that wanting to do well in music leads to wanting to do well elsewhere. When in exceptional cases, difficulties have been encountered, special provision has been made and progress throughout the school has continued. In such cases Schedule 5 of the Awards Regulations can be brought to bear: this states that entry into a music college can be facilitated by the grant of a certificate showing the successful completion of a foundation course in music which has been of at least two years duration.

With the specialism being so dominant and the general education so necessary, a question arises as to whether too many pressures are being exerted on pupils. Each has an individual timetable and virtually every minute of each day is allocated so that maximum advantage can be made of lesson time, practice, and academic tuition. Further, communal living for so wide an age-range from eight to eighteen demands careful regulation, particularly because the school is situated in an inner city area. Is there not a risk that the school has become too claustrophobic?

Working through, and with, change does not put one in a position to answer this question, because only an inside view is possible. An outsider, however, has the advantage of observing things as they are and not the way in which they have evolved, so the opportunity has been taken of inviting outsiders with no previous knowledge of Chetham's to comment on how the school seems today.

We had always worked in schools which specialised in behaviour problems and the difficulties that pupils had had in other social situations. We expected, because of the strong boarding element, something of the introversion characteristic of public schools. . . .

What we found from the first moment, and have had no reason to change our opinion since, was how fulfilled the children are. We were taken aback by their friendliness, and the curiosity and excitement that radiates from being with them. They are such a mixed bunch, from different social backgrounds and temperaments, yet each had their own personal driving force. Having come from schools where there wasn't this sense of purpose, where we were used to children being bored and therefore getting into trouble, this was most noticeable. It makes you feel that children should be strongly encouraged to involve themselves, and to be overworked rather than underworked. We also found that Chetham's is highly tolerant of individual differences. This is hard for any institution to be. By their nature, schools usually create their own social norms and make sure that everyone conforms. It is very difficult to build an institution that is able to tolerate individuals, and this is particularly remarkable at Chetham's in the light of the rapid development of the school. It is a tribute to the headmaster and his management skills in dealing with the diversity of staff and pupils. There's a sense of growth, of positive change and the possibility of an exciting future which you pick up from the pupils. Some of the sixth formers, who have been at Chetham's for several years, say very clearly and without hesitation that the place is improving every year. Talking with the maintenance staff or with the ladies of the laundry, one picks up the same positive, purposeful attitude. Another point is that you can't ignore Manchester. Living right in the middle, you can take advantage of all the remarkable opportunities that a city like this provides. There's a great loosening of any of the claustrophobic feeling which usually clings round a boarding-school.

Chetham's today, then, is beginning to fulfil a need to provide an environment suitable for the fostering of musical ability in children. In the seventeenth century, the need had been to enable children to become apprentices and learn a trade. In subsequent centuries, adaptations have been made to meet with the altering needs of society and the extending nature of education. What has been common to all however, has been the sandstone walls of a medieval college. Amid all of today's speculation about the future, there still remains at Chetham's the calming sense of history.

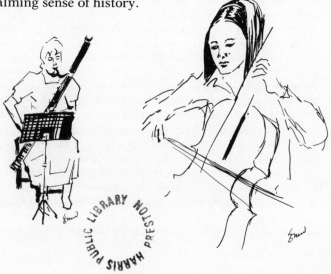

Appendices

1 *The origin of Mr Humprey Chetham's Hospital School and its operation under the terms of the 1651 will.*

'How little of public interest is to be found in the life of a private Merchant,' wrote W. R. Whatton in 1833 as he introduced the first history of Chetham's Hospital School. He had been invited to undertake the work by Dr S. Hibbert who, in turn, had been commissioned by the Manchester publishers, Thomas Agnew and Joseph Zanetti, to write a 'History of the Foundations in Manchester of Christ's College, Chetham's Hospital and the Free Grammar School'. Hibbert had been unable to complete this three-fold work himself because he had been misled as to the amount of research that would be required. The publishers had obtained a transcript from Rev J. Greswell, 'schoolmaster of the Chetham Institution, a gentleman of very great private worth, and a scholar', but Hibbert, to use his own words, was 'doomed to great annoyance' when he found out that Greswell 'had been employed merely in collecting materials, but had not himself, as I began to discover, composed a single line of the history'. So Whatton dealt with Chetham's, while Hibbert limited himself to the Collegiate Church and the Grammar School.

After 1833 further material became available, but it was not until 1892 that arrangements were in hand for a more complete study to be published. Preliminary work was undertaken by Canon F. R. Raines, and after his death in 1878 his work was revised and extended by C.W. Sutton. In 1903, what could be regarded as the official *Life of Humphrey Chetham* was published by the Chetham Society in two volumes. The evidence provided by Raines and Sutton, together with more recent research,[1] throws a different light on Whatton's opinion that

1 C. Haigh, *Reformation and Resistance in Tudor Lancashire* (1975); B. Manning, *The English People and the English Revolution* (1976); B. G. Blackwood, *The Lancashire Gentry and the Great Rebellion* (1978); B. Manning (ed) *Politics, Religion and the English Civil War*.

there was 'little of public interest' in Humphrey Chetham's life: the origins of the school were deeply embedded in the public events of the time.

When Humphrey Chetham was preparing his will in 1651 at the age of seventy one, England had no monarch, Presbyterianism had taken over the Collegiate Church and no agreement had yet been reached between Parliament and the Army as to how the country should be governed. He had been active in events which had led to this crisis, and some of his friends were in prison and were being interrogated. Also in 1651 the Earl of Derby, whose properties were sequestered by Parliament, was executed in Bolton. The will instructed that, if possible, the College buildings which had, since 1549, been Derby property should be purchased so that they could house forty poor boys. To understand the complexities that surrounded the foundation of the school, it would seem necessary to review briefly the life and times of Humphrey Chetham and the problems that surrounded him.

He was the fifth son of Henry and Jane Cheetham, who were engaged in trade, and was twenty-three when his father died in 1603. It was a close-knit family and in 1595 the father had made provision for the maintenance of his younger children by placing £200 in the hands of the eldest son, James, described as a 'clothier living in Salford'. Out of this sum the other children (George, Simon, Humphrey, Ralph and Alice) were each to receive £4 a year, and £40 was to be paid to each child on attaining twenty one years.

George and Humphrey were, in turn, apprenticed to George Tipping, a wealthy linen draper and general merchant. George Chetham[2] settled in London and it was his close collaboration with his younger brother, Humphrey, that led to the prosperous development of the Chetham trading family. In London, the Livery Companies had a monopoly over export but Lancashire families evaded this by having their own agents in the capital city. George was the distributing agent and Humphrey was the supplier, specialising in fustians.

2 The spelling of the surname with one 'e' became standardised in 1635 (see p. 145). To avoid confusion, the name is spelt as in the later version, even though a different spelling was in use before 1635.

These were produced by weaving loosely floating weft picks across a strong warp, completely covering it, and then using a fustian knife to cut the weft floats to produce a pile which would then be brushed, sheared and singed; finally the fabric would be bleached and dyed. Fustians were principally manufactured in Bolton where they were bought 'in the grey by the Manchester chapman (particularly by the benevolent Humphrey Chetham Esq, the founder of the Blue Coat Hospital) who finished them and sold them in the country'. For a time, Humphrey lived in London with his brother, but by 1619 a deed of partnership was drawn up from which it is clear that Humphrey was based in Manchester with George operating the London end of the business. The joint stock was in the region of £10,000.

Humphrey Chetham has been singled out as 'the most successful gentleman merchant of Caroline Lancashire' who between 1620 and 1628 invested £9,800 in land purchase.[3] In 1620 Clayton Hall was purchased from Sir John Byron of Newstead Abbey, and it became Humphrey's permanent residence. In 1628 he acquired the manor of Turton from the Orrell family. He refused to purchase a knighthood under the scheme whereby owners of land valued at over £40 were expected to make a payment, and had preferred to pay the appropriate fine for avoiding what amounted to a disguised tax.

In 1635 he became High Sheriff of the County Palatine, and in the same year, largely through his initiative, Christ's College, Manchester, was closed down and re-established with a new charter. Both events throw light on the difficult position he would be facing when the issues which were to be raised in the civil wars were gathering momentum. He was very much a public figure and, like all public figures, had to face criticism, particularly because he was a member of the merchant class intruding on areas usually the prerogative of the landed aristocracy. He had not wanted to be picked as Sheriff and had pleaded with an officer of the Court of the Duchy of Lancaster to 'stand betwixt me and danger, and if any put me forward, that you will stand in the way and suffer me not to come in

3 B. G. Blackwood, *The Lancashire Gentry and the Great Rebellion* (Chetham Society, Third Series, vol. 35, 1978) p. 18.

the rank of those that shall be presented to the King's view; whereby I shall be made more popular, and thereby more subject to the peril of hereafter times'.[4] He did not want to be 'more popular', i.e. openly involved in politics, because of the increasing hostility to the King's government. During his year as Sheriff he was to supervise two collections of Ship-money, a tax which was strongly resisted because it had not been authorized by Parliament. He set about this unpopular task in a practical manner, and, with his customary thoroughness, the two payments of £2,200 and £3,500 were duly collected and transferred to the Treasurer of the Navy.

Not only was the tax collection unpleasant and arduous, but Chetham had to face an accusation of wrongfully withholding some of the money collected. It was alleged that he had put £96 aside, and in a letter to the Chancellor of the Duchy of Lancaster Chetham gave a detailed account of why this amount had been withheld. He claimed that the money was to cover any contingencies should there be disparities between an assessment based on the book of rates and what was actually collected. He also stated that the money had still not been sent to London because of the danger of thefts in transport. 'I have made bold sincerely to inform your Lordships of the truth, lest being so traduced by these whispering suggestors by my silence your Lordship might think I wanted matter truly to allege in my own defence.'[5]

Another unpleasantness arose when armorial bearings were needed for the banners and flags used for the traditional ceremonies associated with the office of Sheriff. The Chetham family of Crumpsall had no entitlement to bear arms and there was much jealousy and envy when Humphrey took office. 'I perceive that some malicious knaves have endeavoured to disgrace you about your coat of arms', reported Richard Johnson, who undertook to secure official approval in London. To step upwards out of your class was something which would be scorned and attacked by others, and a proceeding began whose purpose was to prevent the grant of a coat of arms. Through

4 F. R. Raines and C. W. Sutton, *Life of Humphrey Chetham* (Chetham Society, New Series, vol. 49, 1903) p. 74.
5 Raines and Sutton, *op. cit.*, p. 84.

bribery and influence the Heralds' College finally gave permission, and it was at this stage that the standardisation of the spelling of the name 'Chetham' was put into practice. Before 1635 the name had been spelt in five different ways, with the spelling giving the long 'e' in pronounciation, but after 1635 the spelling was 'with two h's and one e', the 'e' in the first syllable being long.[6]

Richard Johnson, who had played an important part in the matter of the coat of arms, had become a Fellow at Christ's College, Manchester, in 1632 and he was also to serve as Humphrey's London agent in drawing the attention of the Privy Council to the neglect of the College by its Warden, Richard Murray. Tithes, the Church tax intended for the upkeep and maintenance of the Collegiate Church, had been leased out for fees which were collected by Chetham and transmitted to Murray, but Murray used the money for his own purposes. Nothing was being done to maintain the fabric of the Church or to meet all the needs of the Fellows. The main difficulty was that the 1578 Charter had provided special rights for the Warden which gave him legal protection. Johnson received instructions from Chetham to employ counsel to draw attention to the damage suffered by the College and to expose the unscrupulousness of Murray in neglecting the responsibilities of a Warden. The outcome was the dismissal of Murray and the termination of the 1578 Charter. A fresh Charter was introduced in 1635 which restricted the power of future Wardens.[7]

In 1635, Humphrey Chetham was fifty-five years old. He was one of the wealthiest landowners in the area; he was also Sheriff for the year and had been the chief instigator for the removal of Warden Murray. In the vital question of where he stood in relation to the issues which were to be raised in the civil wars, there can be little doubt that he sided with the radical element in Manchester. He could well have become a Calvinist. His close relationship with the Fellows of the College (two of whom, Richard Johnson and John Tilsley, were to be

6 Raines and Sutton, *op. cit.*, p.101.
7 Chetham was empowered by the Privy Council 'to take custody of the tithes as the farmer or receiver', which he did until 1639 when John Leigh took over as 'the Bailiff for the College'.

named in his will), would seem to confirm this. Of one of the Fellows, William Bourne, it was recorded that 'seldom or never did he ascend the pulpit but he struck at some popish doctrine before he came down. He dissented little or nothing from the discipline used in Scotland.' Richard Heyricke, who replaced Murray as Warden in 1635, became a Presbyterian during the civil war period. Richard Johnson made his views known in a letter dated 25 August 1635: 'But the idolatry and superstition of the Church of Rome I hate, and I abhor the Doctrine of free will or rather of self-will: and if his Grace (Archbishop Laud) calls this a peevish disposition against the Chuirch, he is not much deceived in me, wheresoever he learned it. I am in God's hands, so is he, and that is my comfort.'

Johnson was to be instructed later, in Humphrey Chetham's will, to purchase 'godly English books, such as Calvins, Prestons and Perkins works'. Perkins had been the charismatic puritan at Cambridge whose sermons had fired the puritan cause and, when printed, had become an important part of Calvinist training. Today in Chetham's Library there stands the Gorton chest containing the books purchased by Johnson in accordance with the instructions in the will. The evidence suggests that Humphrey Chetham was not a supporter of the Arminianism of Archbishop Laud.

Even so, it may be an oversimplification to regard his acceptance in 1643 of the post of Treasurer for the County of Lancaster 'to whom all Moneys collected for the maintenance of soldiers shall be paid' as a clear cut decision to oppose monarchy. When, in September 1642, Lord Strange, the head of the house of Stanley on the retirement of his father the Earl of Derby, had advanced on Manchester with about two thousand five hundred men and seven cannon, the landed gentry came with their tenants to assist the town. The people of Manchester were defending their property against marauding soldiers rather than taking a definite stance against the King. Humphrey Chetham's name does not appear in contemporary accounts, as does that of Thomas Chetham of Nuthurst, as one of the land-owning gentry opposed to the Derby Faction. Maybe he was one of the waverers hoping for a negotiated peace. When offered the post of Treasurer he at first demurred, giving ill health as a reason, but in the end his petition was not accepted, for it was a dangerous time to refuse office. For the next six years he undertook the difficult task of securing and distributing money needed for the taking over of Lancashire by Parliamentary trooops and resisting demands from some commanders which were in excess of what was ordained by deputy lieutenants.

When he was sixty-eight years old and suffering from ill health he received a second summons to be Sheriff, only this time not from the monarch but from Parliament. The scene was being set for the trial of Charles I. Chetham did not want the appointment but seemed unable to secure a cancellation on grounds of ill health. His London agent reported: 'Wednesday last (all those of our Lancashire Parliament men who would have been very ready to have served you therein) with many others to the number of seventy more, were by the Army taken prisoners and expelled the house, so that the City is now in a very sad distraction, and every man enforced to fly thence for his own safety'.[8] Richard Johnson was also acting on Chetham's behalf in London: 'I went to Mr Maynard a Parliament man. . . who tells me he hopes if you have not interested enemies to move against you, I mean who are afraid of the place themselves, we may get you off. . . We will do what we can, be of good cheer. I think you may with conscience , being so old and weak and broken with cares, plead want of ability in memory and quick understanding, show us in brief words what you can truly say for yourself, and think upon some rich man, and great man, that is likely for the place' (5 December 1648).[9]

It was difficult to be of good cheer in Clayton while decisions were being made in London. January came, the King was executed, and still there was no news that an alternative Sheriff had been appointed. Another appeal was made in February: 'My case is this. I am almost seventy years of age, of a very weak constitution; I am not able to get on horseback or light but as I am helped by another, nor being on horseback to ride two miles but with extreme pain and grief, for my particular

8 Raines and Sutton, *op. cit.*, p. 161.
9 Raines and Sutton, *op. cit.*, p. 164.

infirmity increaseth so upon me that it will shortly bring me to my grave: which being sensible of I have for this half year and more confined myself for the most part to my own house and to my chamber: and now this office being put upon me by Parliament through the information of our country gent. either out (of) spleen in those that know my condition, or out of ignorance thereof in others.'[10]

It was a dangerous time to have enemies and refusal to be Sheriff could possibly be interpreted as a refusal to support the decisions being made in London by the Army. On the other hand, Chetham may have been exaggerating the fear that others, jealous of his success in trade and social status, were hoping for his downfall. In a letter to John Bretland who was his main supporter in Parliament he sent a medical certificate 'from Mr Minshull my physician, if either you or Mr Brereton can make use of it, pray do so, if not I would desire you bring it back with you'.[11] In March 1649 came the news that a new Sheriff had been appointed. Chetham was now able to give his attention to another matter which surprisingly was to cause him to withdraw a proposal to make a hospital in the College buildings.

In March 1648, he had secretly approached the Earl of Derby's agent about the possible purchase of the buildings which had been sequestered by Parliament: 'let me enjoin you secrecy to all men but my Lord... I am purposing, and (if God's goodness permit not the wickedness of the wars or some other extraordinary accident to hinder it) am resolved to make an hospital at Manchester; and for that purpose have thought the College a fit place, and considering the uselessness of it to his Lordship in time of peace, much more now being seques-tered, a great part of it spoiled and ruined and become like a dunghill.' The approach was made to the Earl of Derby, and not directly to the Parliamentary Commissioners, because he was contemplating a long-term arrangement, not one limited to the interim period of sequestration. In time, the local com-mittee of Sequestrators was approached for permission to buy the buildings 'to be employed for a pious use, viz. for an habita

10 Raines and Sutton, *op. cit.*, p. 164-5.
11 Raines and Sutton, *op. cit.*, p. 173.

tion for some poor children, or aged and infirm old folks, which he intended to maintain and provide for at his own cost and charges'. The Committee was prepared to agree until one of them, Thomas Birch, produced a less general, more specific commitment which Chetham was asked to endorse. Birch wanted the number of old people to be specified (i.e. twenty) and also the amount of annual payment to be made to the old people and the young boys to be stated. Chetham refused and withdrew the application. The intervention of Birch has been interpreted as expressing a distrust of Chetham's intentions: 'When Mr Chetham saw them (the Birch proposals) he was so much offended that Mr Birch should have been so lordly to command over so charitable an institution: And therefore did refuse to buy the College'.[12]

Two years later, in 1651, when the will was being prepared, old people were not to be included in the Hospital, a change which would seem unusual in that it was traditional for wealthy benefactors to make provision for the elderly and infirm. George Chetham, Humphrey's brother, who had died in 1626 leaving the bulk of his estate to Humphrey, had given instruction in his will for 'black frize coats' to be given to fifty poor men 'all of them to be of age of three score years or more and none of them under the age of fifty years'.[13] Although Humphrey, in his previous wills had followed his brother's example in providing for old people, the final 1651 will concentrated on provision only for the young. Possibly the change was made because of his experience in maintaining twenty-two poor boys who were housed with five or six families since 1649. If the number were to be increased to forty, a careful financier like Chetham may have wanted to ensure that sufficient money would be available to provide for continuity and in the calculation help for the elderly had to be sacrificed. Also, possibly, his experience as a trader may have drawn attention to the need for a supply of good apprentices. In a previous cancelled will, dated 1636, no mention was made of apprenticing poor

12 Raines and Sutton, *op. cit.*, pp. 194-5.
13 The fifty were to be from some of the parishes from which boys were to be selected in accordance with Humphrey's will: 15 from Manchester, 15 from Salford, 10 from Crumpsall, 5 from Droylsden and 5 from Failsworth.

boys but only of helping the elderly. Another cancelled will of 1642 spoke of a relatively small grant of £50 for poor scholars in addition to help for the poor.

Humphrey Chetham died on 20 September 1653, and the funeral took place on 11 October. As was usual at that time, funeral expenses were high.[14] The order of procession for the funeral began: 'First, forty boys in blew cotes, which he did mantayne, two and two houlding pencills', marching two by two carrying staffs on the top of which were pennons carrying the motto of the deceased: 'Quod Tuum Tene'. The apparel worn by the boys was the Blue Coat uniform common to other charity schools.

The Parliamentary Committee of Sequestration had let the College buildings to Joseph Werden, who in turn had sub-let part to Presbyterians, and another part to a congregation of Independents whose minister was a captain in the parliamentary army. Humphrey Chetham's will stipulated that £500 should be used to purchase a house for the boys: 'that the same poor boys may cohabit, and live together in one house, or two, as may be thought convenient. . . . And my desire is, that the great house, with the buildings, out-houses, courts, yards, gardens and appurtenances in Manchester aforesaid, called the college, or the college house, may be purchased, and bought for the same purpose, (if it may be had, and obtained upon good terms and for a good estate).' In January 1654 an offer of £350 was made but it was turned down. The cost of rehabilitating the neglected College buildings could well have exceeded the £500 total stipulated in the will, and consideration was given to buying or building some other property for the boys. The lessee then changed his mind, was willing to accept £400, and agreement was reached on 2 August 1654, whereby the executors of Humphrey Chetham obtained 'all that capital messuage or mansion house with appurtenances called the College'. Repairs and alterations were carried out so that the forty boys and the Library could be accommodated. The daytime rooms of the priests in the cloisters became places for the teaching and domestic staff, while the priests' dormi-

14 £1161 19s 6d. Raines and Sutton, *op. cit.*, Appendix III, pp. 278-301, reproduces the expenditure in considerable detail.

tories were adapted to house the books of the Library. The Warden's retiring room became the Library Reading Room, while his daytime room below became an Audit Room where accounts were to be regularly presented and examined. On 5 August 1656, 'the Hospital boys were removed from their several private quarters, where they had been tabled, in the Hospital, and lodged there.'

Humphrey's nephews, George and Edward Chetham, were appointed executors and instructed to purchase £7,000 of lands which were to be conveyed to twenty-four named feoffees on the understanding that 'the whole clear profits, issues, benefits and revenues thereof. . . shall and may, to the pleasure of Almighty God, be ordered, disposed of, employed, and converted, for and about the relief, maintenance, education, bringing up, and binding apprentice, or other preferment of so many, and such poor boys or male children'. The annual revenue of £420 was to be used so that forty boys could be 'sufficiently maintained and kept with meat, drink, lodging and apparel, and also educated and brought up to learning or labour in the towns of Manchester and Salford'. At the age of fourteen they would be 'put forth apprentice to some honest masters, or otherwise preferred', although boys from the Bolton area were not to be bound apprentice in Manchester. The boys were to be drawn from a restricted area of parishes where the Chetham family had interests or connections. Fifteen were from the Bolton area (Bolton ten, Turton five), and twenty-five from the Manchester area (Manchester fourteen, Salford six, Droylsden three, Crumpsall two), and a strict injunction was issued that the proportion from each parish should not be exceeded.

These conditions were to be substantially operative for the next three hundred years. Revenues were to increase to allow one hundred boys to benefit from the endowment in the nineteenth century. The twenty-four feoffees responsible for the financing and running of the Hospital School and the Library, which were administered separately, came from important families in the Manchester district. When one died, it became customary for the replacement to come from the same locality. The original selection must have been made on the basis of friendship and reliability rather than on the sectarian lines that characterised the 1650s. Some were Presbyterian, some were Royalist and some were Catholics. John Tilsley, a renowned Presbyterian who supported the execution of the Earl of Derby in 1651 and was to be ejected from his living in 1662, continued to serve as a feoffee until his death in 1684 when his place was, ironically, to be taken up by the next earl of Derby.

The restoration of the monarchy in 1660 and the subsequent imposition of Anglicanism throughout England may have necessitated some modification of the Nonconformist elements which had characterised the thinking behind Humphrey Chetham's will. In 1661, a charter of incorporation 'for the better ordering, governing and managing' was sought, and in 1665 such a charter was granted at Oxford by Charles II. The feoffees were henceforth to be knowns as 'Governors of the Hospital and Library' and they were, and still are, required to take the oath of allegiance and supremacy. Religious considerations did not prevent a Presbyterian like John Tilsley from taking the oath in 1666. The return of monarchy and the Church of England had produced a more stable situation than when the will was being prepared in 1651.

Also with the Restoration, negotiations followed about the College buildings which in the civil wars period had been sequestered from the Derby family. The outcome was a payment of £70 to the Countess Dowager of Derby. The revenues and disbursements of the Hospital and Library were supervised by one of the feoffees who took on the office of Treasurer. The first Treasurer was Thomas Minshull, apothecary, who had in 1648 provided the medical certificate showing that Humphrey Chetham was too ill to undertake for a second time the duties of Sheriff. Minshull himself when he died in 1689 followed Humphrey's example, and bequeathed a charity which enabled poor boys to be apprenticed as apothecaries.

A petition would be made for admission to the Hospital School. Taking, for example, a petition dated 5 September 1857, the details indicate how strictly the terms of the will were being followed. The boy had to have been christened in one of the named parishes 'and not elsewhere', he had to be 'above six and under ten years', and it had to be certified that he was the son of 'honest, industrious and painful Parents, and not wandering or idle beggars or rogues, and is not a bastard, nor lame, infirm or diseased'. Information is provided about the family circumstances. The petitioning mother, who cannot sign her name but makes her mark instead, is a widow with nine children under the age of fifteen. The eldest boy earns 6s a week, while she earns 3s a week. 'The Father when living sought earnestly to maintain his large family honestly and bring them up in the paths of virtue. He was a diligent Sunday School teacher to the last.' All petitions concluded with the words: 'Your Petitioner, therefore, prays that you will elect the said poor boy into your Hospital, and admit him to partake of the Charity so far as you shall deem him worthy according to the Rules thereof.' The information was certified as correct by two Churchwardens and an Overseer of the Poor.

The first 'Keeper of the Library' was Richard Johnson who had performed useful services to Humphrey Chetham, and Richard Dutton was the first 'Master of the children in the said Hospital'. Information is lacking about what exactly was taught in the early stages of the school, but from press adver-tisements in the eighteenth century, it would seem that, in addition to basic instruction in reading, writing and book-keeping, senior boys could be employed in contract work while still at school. The will had made specific provision for this contingency by allowing boys to receive 'the profits of such easy labour, as they shall be set unto, to keep them from idle-ness, during such time as they shall be between ten and four-teen years of age'. *The Manchester Mercury* of 15 October 1765 invited proposals for 'any person who is willing to instruct and employ any number of the Blue Boys in Spinning Twine, Candlewick, or in any other easy Business or Employment'. Two years later, some of the boys were engaged in shoe-making, and in 1767 another advertisement in the *Manchester Mercury* (5 June 1767) asked for an instructor 'of good Charac-ter for Honesty, Sobriety and Diligence' to teach the boys how to wind cotton and worsted yarn. The hours of work were 'from eight to twelve in the forenoon, and one to four in the after-noon'. The announcement was made that 'there is a room provided in the College for the Boys to work in, and Wheels will be provided by the Trustees. The Number of Boys to be constantly employed will be Thirty'. By then, there were eighty boys in the Hospital. Profits obtained through employment were put aside and paid later to individual boys as a bonus on the successful completion of an apprenticeship. The Hospital was not exploiting child labour, but carrying out Humphrey Chetham's intention that boys should be 'kept out of idleness'.

The exploitation of pauper apprentices has received much attention from novelists and historians, but the Hospital situation was exceptional because the boys were not 'pauper' in the sense of being dependent on parish relief, and care was taken by the governors to ensure that only reliable tradesmen undertook the provision of apprenticeship on a boy's leaving at the age of fourteen. In 1751 an indenture was made for a boy to 'Learn the Art Trade and Mystery of a Taylor', and for the next seven years he had to serve his master, 'his secrets keep, his Lawful Commands Gladly everywhere obey, he shall do no damage to his said Master, nor see it to be done by others without Letting or giving Notice thereof to his said Master, he shall not waste his said Master's Goods, nor lend them Unlawfully to any, he shall not Comitt Fornication nor contract Matrimony within the said Term, at Cards, Dice, or any other Unlawful Games he shall not play, whereby his said Master may have Damage, he shall not absent himself Day or Night from his said Master's Service without his Leave, nor frequent Alehouses, Taverns or Play Houses but in all things behave himself as a faithfull Apprentice ought to during the said Term'.

This was standard practice, and the Hospital provided £4 for each indenture. The Master Tailor in return had to 'cause the said Apprentice to be taught and instructed in the Art, Trade and Mystery of a Taylor', and 'provide and Give unto the said apprentice good and sufficient Meat Drink washing and Lodging Apparel both Linens and Woollens and all other Necessaries fit for his Degree and Calling during the said Term of seven Years', with a penalty of £8 if these conditions were not carried out. The importance of the apprenticeship system for a school leaver was the degree of security it provided.

In 1816 there were sixteen school leavers from the Hospital. Six went into work connected with mills (two weavers, a fustian-dyer, a cork-cutter, a pattern and copper-plate printer, and a millwright and machine-maker), four went into housing (a plumber, a joiner and carpenter, an upholsterer and cabinet-maker), one became a sailor because England was then at war with France, and the remaining five were apprenticed to the service industries (hatter, shoe-maker, basket-maker, confectioner and a distiller). The apprentice distiller was George Pilkington who rose to eminence in Manchester, endowing many charities himself and providing for a statue of Humphrey Chetham to be set up in Manchester Cathedral. He was the prototype 'Manchester Man' of the novel by Mrs Linnaeus Banks in which he makes one or two brief appearances in a subsidiary role.

The type of apprenticeship undertaken by school leavers remained virtually unchanged until railway and industrial change brought in a different demand. Of the nineteen leavers in 1838, ten were in industry (a whip and thong-maker, two machine-makers, two whitesmiths,[15] three spindle-makers and a brush-maker) and among the others were two stone-masons and a letter-press printer. Office work made its appearance in 1854 with two boys being apprenticed as warehousemen and clerks. Of the fourteen boys who left in 1892, only two went directly into industry while eight became clerks (described as railway, solicitor's, builder's, telegraph and shorthand); one boy was apprenticed to be a teacher, another to a bookseller.

In 1888 a booklet, *Manchester of Today*, was published which was designed to attract to the city 'Business Men and Commercial Interests'. Chetham's had this mention: 'That an excellent work is done by the income of the charity is not open to question. But the £4 apprenticeship fee, some people think, might perhaps be exchanged with advantage for scholarships to enable boys who manifest special ability to prolong their studies, while nothing would be lost if the obsolete and inconvenient dress were replaced by garments of more modern fashion.' These changes did not take place until 1952.

15 'Whitesmith' = a worker in 'whiteiron', a tinsmith.

2 *School uniform*

The Blue Coat uniform, traditional to Hospital Schools, was worn as directed by Humphrey Chetham's will and consisted of a long outer garment of blue cloth, an under-petticoat of yellow, blue worsted stockings, a blue flat cap and a pair of white linen bands. Constant attention was given to the health of the boys and by the nineteenth century, when the number of boys had increased (forty in 1656, sixty in 1665, eighty in 1779, and one hundred in 1826), a surgeon's report drew attention to the disadvantages of wearing a petticoat. 'The loose adaptation of a petticoat form of dress to all the surface of the Body renders it equally a source of skin disease at each season of the year, in summer from constant irritation of the skin by particles of dust and in winter by its deficiency of warmth preventing cutaneous exhalation. In consequence of the want of circulation in the extremities, frost-bites are not unfrequent and trivial cuts and abrasions which in more robust constitutions rapidly heal become in them very troublesome ulcers. I have brought these cases prominently before you because they admit of an easy remedy in the substitution of undergarments fitting more closely to the Body than the present yellow petticoat and by an arrangement which shall cause each boy of delicate constitution to be furnished with a flannel waiscot [*sic*] during the winter months' (1845).

Petticoats went out and trousers came in. In 1896 it was decided that 'in future the boys be dressed in blue cloth knee breeches instead of corduroy and cloth trousers, that yellow stockings be worn for full dress, and blue stockings for Half Dress, that the long coat be worn as at present with the addition of a leather belt, that a blue jacket, and that low shoes with buckles be worn instead of the present Blucher shoes'. Authority was given to purchase a hundred suits 'to consist of serge coat, blue beaver breeches and cap of same material for the sum of £90, and two hundred pairs of two-buckle shoes as per sample and to keep same in repair for twelve months for the sum of £200'. Breeches were replaced in 1934 under certain conditions: '1. That blue shorts and turn-down stockings be provided for all boys to wear on weekdays and only within the precincts of the Hospital. 2. That shorts be permitted to be worn in conjunction with the blue jersey but not in conjuction with the tunic. 3. That all shorts be withdrawn from the boys prior to their leaving for holidays.'

This is substantially the dress still worn today by some of the resident boys on ceremonial occasions such as Founder's Day: long coat, short trousers, yellow stockings, blue cloth tunic with brass buttons, buckled shoes and white lined Genevan band round the neck.

3 *Visitors*

The College buildings which date from 1421 are a unique example of medieval architecture and have always attracted notice. In the nineteenth century, however, not only the buildings but also a miscellaneous collection of bric-à-brac attracted the curiosity of visitors. It was put on display in the Library, which was out of bounds for the boys, but one of the senior trades of a boy was to act as a guide and move visitors round as quickly as possible. There were set times when the College would be open to the public and a charge was made which went to Hospital funds, and woe betide any boy who dared to secrete a coin for himself.

A list, dated 1913, of the curiosities that were on show, has survived, and the list is identical with the one included in Henn's *Memoir of Richard Hanby*, who had served as House Governor, and published in 1886. Even earlier, in 1839, attention was being drawn to the ritual involved when a visit to Chetham's was being made. The first extract is from the guidebook '*Manchester as it is:* or notice of the Institutions, Manufactures, Commerce, Railways, etc, of the *Metropolis of Manufacturers*', due allowance being made for the pomposity and verboseness of the description, and then follows the list of curiosities.

> The visitor having entered the yard, will do well to inquire for a guide, when a juvenile cicerone will be summoned by a bell. The guides are a privileged class, and are duly trained by their own fraternity, to the right performance of their functions. With little

preliminary ceremony, they usher the visitor into an apartment, in which he is directed to look here, and gaze there: at sundry wonderful objects. As if it were profanity to linger too long on any one object in particular, the worthy guide makes a quick transition from one to another; and the curious stranger, if he gets a hasty glance, must subdue all further curiosity. The taciturnity of the youthful guide on all subjects not in the catalogue of curiosities, forbids any question in search of explanation, and his imperturbable gravity seems impossible to relax itself into the further approximation to a smile, even when he points to the 'cock that crows when he smells roast beef'. Like the priests of the Delphic Apollo, he appears to have imbibed a peculiar inspiration to fit him for the high duties of his office, and as long as he is officiating its influence remains. After exploring the various galleries and the Library, the visitor may descend into the College buttery and taste the wheaten bread, and take a draught of the wholesome ale, which form a solid foundation for the boys to build a good meal upon.

The 'catalogue of curiosities' is reproduced in Henn's *Memoir of Richard Hanby* (1886), and is the same as a list used by a boy who, in 1913, was carrying out the duties of guide. The charge of 6*d* was duly recorded and annual statements were made of the total revenue resulting from visits. The display seems to have been discontinued after the First World War, and the visit put on a more formal footing, with official times for parties to inspect the dormitories and see the Library without the oddities previously on show.

That's a snake.
Over its back are two watch-bills.
Those four are Ancient Swords.
That sword, with a white haft, once belonged to General Wolffe.
That top one is an Alligator.
That bottom one is a Crocodile.
Those two Colours were carried by the Manchester Volunteers at the Siege of Gibraltar in 1782.
That top one with a white face is a Monkey.
At the right side of the Monkey there is a green Lizard.
At the left side of the Monkey a land Tortoise.
That black one is part of a Whale's bone,
That flat one is a Tortoise.
That, as if it were creeping down the wall, is a brown Lizard.
At the side of the Lizard, there is a Dog-fish.

Over the Dog-fish, there is a young Ass's Jawbone.

At the side of the Ass's jawbone, there is a Porpoise's skull.

That Bow and those Arrows once belonged to the North American, or Dog-rib'd Indians.

That long thing at the bottom is the Skin of a Snake.

At the side of the backbone of a shark there is Oliver Cromwell's sword.

At the side of the sword, there are two coconut shells.

At the side of the Shells, there is a Porpoise's skull.

Over the skull there is a Turtle.

At the side of the Turtle there is a Sea Hen.

At the side of the Sea Hen there is the fin of a Shark.

That top one is an American Weed.

Under the Weed, there is an Alligator.

At the end of its mouth there is part of an old woman's clog, that was split by a thunderbolt, and she was not hurt.

Under the Alligator there is a Crocodile.

At the end of its tail there is the Snow Shoe of a Laplander.

Over its last leg there is a Turtle's head.

Over its belly there is the Fin of a Unicorn fish.

At the end of its mouth there is part of a young Shark's jaw-bone.

That in the small frame is the skeleton of a Nightingale.

And that is the skeleton of a Man.

This Table was cut and carved so queer that it contains as many pieces of wood as there are days in the year – 365.

That's an Indian basket, and that's the fin of a Sword-fish.

That's the head of a wild Albatross.

That Gun was taken from the dead body of a Frenchman at the Battle of Waterloo in the year 1815.

That is part of Oliver Cromwell's stone.

Those are two Indian Nuts.

That is the Skeleton of a male child.

That is the Hand of an Egyptian Mummy.

That Boot once belonged to Queen Elizabeth.

Those two pieces of wood were Almanacks, before printing was invented.

That's a piece of Roman Pottery, found in Castle Field in the year 1728.

That's part of a Shield, found in Castle Field in the same year.

That's the haft of the Whip that killed the Snake.

That's a Hippopotamus' double tooth.

That's its single tooth.

That's an ancient Stilletto, or Spanish Dagger.

Those two are a pair of American Snow Shoes.

That top one is a Hairy Man.

Under the Hairy Man is a Leathern Bag.

Under the Leathern bag is a Shark's Mouth.

At the side of the Hairy Man's left leg there's the backbone of a Shark.

That is the picture of Mr Thyer, one of the late Librarians of this College.

That is a picture of Humphrey Chetham's nephew; his name was James Chetham.

That is a gift to Humphrey Chetham Esq 1655.

That is a picture of Wm. Whittaker, the distinguished Martyr.

That is a picture of Alexander Nowell, one of the late Deans in St. Paul's Church, London.

That is a Picture of the first Minister who ever preached in Manchester Cathedral: his name was Robt. Bolton – born in Blackburn.

This Clock used to strike once a year, presented by Nicholas Clegg, 1695.

That is a picture of John Bradford, Martyr under Queen Mary.

That is a picture of the Right Honourable Richard Bootle Wilbraham, late Member of Parliament.

That is a picture of the late Earl of Wilton.

That Cock crows when it smells roast beef.

That is a picture of Wilbraham Egerton Esq.

That is a picture of Carlos Lawson, late Head Grammar School Master.

That is a picture of Humphrey Chetham Esq., Founder of this Hospital, and those are his Coat of Arms.

That is a picture of the Rev James Lloyd, later Rector of Radcliffe.

That is a picture of Sir Joseph Radcliffe.

That is the shape of a Pelican pecking its breast, and feeding its young out of its own blood:

That's the way out.